W9-BVT-303

PN
6110
.C4
P3
1971

PATMORE

The childre...

from the be...

ILLINOIS CENTRAL COLLEGE
PN6110.C4P3 1971
STACKS
The children's garland from the bes

A12900 503333

Withdrawn

Illinois Central College
Learning Resources Center

GRANGERS

THE
CHILDREN'S GARLAND

THE

CHILDREN'S GARLAND

FROM THE BEST POETS

SELECTED AND ARRANGED BY
COVENTRY *KERSEY DIGHTON* PATMORE, *1823-1896, Comp.*

Granger Index Reprint Series

ILLINOIS CENTRAL COLLEGE
LEARNING RESOURCES CENTER

BOOKS FOR LIBRARIES PRESS
FREEPORT, NEW YORK

45219

PN
6110
.C4
P3
1971

First Published 1862
Reprinted 1971

INTERNATIONAL STANDARD BOOK NUMBER:
0-8369-6283-4

LIBRARY OF CONGRESS CATALOG CARD NUMBER:
73-167478

PRINTED IN THE UNITED STATES OF AMERICA

PREFACE

THIS volume will, I hope, be found to contain
nearly all the genuine poetry in our language
fitted to please children, — of and from the age at
which they have usually learned to read, — in common
with grown people. A collection of this sort has, I
believe, never before been made, although its utility
seems clear.

The test applied, in every instance, in the work of
selection, has been that of having actually pleased intelligent children ; and my object has been to make a
book which shall be to them no more nor less than a
book of equally good poetry is to intelligent grown
persons. The charm of such a book to the latter class
of readers is rather increased than lessened by the sur-
mised existence in it of an unknown amount of power,
meaning, and beauty, beyond that which is at once to
be seen ; and children will not like this volume the
less because, though it contains little or nothing which
will not at once please and amuse them, it also con-

tains much, the full excellence of which it will be long before most of them are able to understand.

The application of the above test has excluded nearly all verse written expressly for children, and most of the poetry written about children for grown people. Hence the absence of several well-known pieces, which some persons who examine this volume may be surprised at not finding in it.

I have taken the liberty of omitting portions of a few poems, which would else have been too long or otherwise unsuitable for the collection ; and, in a very few instances, I have ventured to substitute a word or a phrase, when that of the author has made the piece in which it occurs unfit for children's reading. The abbreviations I have been compelled to make in the " Ancient Mariner," in order to bring that poem within the limits of this collection, are so considerable as to require particular mention and apology.

No translations have been inserted but such as, by their originality of style and modification of detail, are entitled to stand as original poems.

COVENTRY PATMORE.

December, 1861.

CONTENTS

THE CHILDREN'S GARLAND

THE CHILD AND THE PIPER

PIPING down the valleys wild,
    Piping songs of pleasant glee,
On a cloud I saw a child,
    And he, laughing, said to me,

'Pipe a song about a lamb,'
    So I piped with merry cheer;
'Piper, pipe that song again,'
    So I piped, he wept to hear.

'Drop thy pipe, thy happy pipe,
    Sing thy songs of happy cheer.'
So I sang the same again,
    While he wept with joy to hear.

'Piper, sit thee down and write
    In a book that all may read.'
So he vanish'd from my sight;
    And I pluck'd a hollow reed,

And I made a rural pen,
   And I stain'd the water clear,
And I wrote my happy songs
   Every child may joy to hear.
                  W. Blake

II

ON MAY MORNING

NOW the bright morning star, day's harbinger,
   Comes dancing from the east, and leads with her
The flow'ry May, who from her green lap throws
The yellow cowslip, and the pale primrose.
   Hail, bounteous May, that doth inspire
   Mirth and youth and warm desire !
   Woods and groves are of thy dressing,
   Hill and dale doth boast thy blessing.
Thus we salute thee with our early song,
And welcome thee, and wish thee long.
                  J. Milton

III

THE APPROACH OF THE FAIRIES

NOW the hungry lion roars,
   And the wolf behowls the moon ;
  Whilst the heavy ploughman snores,
   All with weary task foredone.
  Now the wasted brands do glow,
   Whilst the scritch owl, scritching loud,

Puts the wretch that lies in woe
   In remembrance of a shroud.
Now it is the time of night
   That the graves, all gaping wide,
Every one lets forth his sprite,
   In the churchway paths to glide :
And we fairies, that do run,
   By the triple Hecate's team,
From the presence of the sun,
   Following darkness like a dream,
Now are frolic ; not a mouse
Shall disturb this hallowed house :
I am sent with broom before,
To sweep the dust behind the door.

Through the house give glimmering light ;
   By the dead and drowsy fire,
Every elf and fairy sprite
   Hop as light as bird from brier ;
And this ditty after me,
Sing and dance it trippingly.
First rehearse this song by rote,
To each word a warbling note,
Hand in hand, with fairy grace,
We will sing, and bless this place.

W. Shakespeare

IV

ANSWER TO A CHILD'S QUESTION

DO you ask what the birds say? The sparrow, the dove,
The linnet, and thrush say ' I love, and I love !'
In the winter they 're silent, the wind is so strong ;
What it says I don't know, but it sings a loud song.
But green leaves, and blossoms, and sunny warm weather,
And singing and loving — all come back together.
But the lark is so brimful of gladness and love,
The green fields below him, the blue sky above,
That he sings, and he sings, and forever sings he,
' I love my Love, and my Love loves me.'

S. T. Coleridge

V

THE BROOK

I COME from haunts of coot and hern,
    I make a sudden sally,
And sparkle out among the fern,
    To bicker down a valley.

By thirty hills I hurry down,
    Or slip between the ridges,
By twenty thorps, a little town,
    And half a hundred bridges.

Till last by Philip's farm I flow
   To join the brimming river,
For men may come, and men may go,
   But I go on forever.

I chatter over stony ways,
   In little sharps and trebles,
I bubble into eddying bays,
   I babble on the pebbles.

With many a curve my bank I fret
   By many a field and fallow,
And many a fairy foreland set
   With willow-weed and mallow.

I chatter, chatter, as I flow
   To join the brimming river,
For men may come, and men may go,
   But I go on forever.

I wind about, and in and out,
   With here a blossom sailing,
And here and there a lusty trout,
   And here and there a grayling,

And here and there a foamy flake
   Upon me as I travel,
With many a silvery waterbreak
   Above the golden gravel,

And draw them all along and flow
   To join the brimming river,
For men may come, and men may go,
   But I go on forever.

I steal by lawns and grassy plots,
  I slide by hazel covers,
I move the sweet forget-me-nots
  That grow for happy lovers.

I slip, I slide, I gloom, I glance,
  Among my skimming swallows ;
I make the netted sunbeam dance
  Against my sandy shallows.

I murmur under moon and stars
  In brambly wildernesses ;
I linger by my shingly bars ;
  I loiter round my cresses ;

And out again I curve and flow
  To join the brimming river,
For men may come, and men may go,
  But I go on forever.

                            A. Tennyson

VI

STARS

THEY glide upon their endless way,
  Forever calm, forever bright ;
No blind hurry, no delay,
  Mark the Daughters of the Night :
They follow in the track of Day,
  In divine delight.

Shine on, sweet orbed Souls, for aye,
  Forever calm, forever bright :

We ask not whither lies your way,
  Nor whence ye came, nor what your light.
Be — still a dream throughout the day,
  A blessing through the night.

                              B. Cornwall

VII

THE SHEPHERD TO HIS LOVE

COME live with me and be my Love,
  And we will all the pleasures prove
That hills and valleys, dale and field,
And all the craggy mountains yield.

There will we sit upon the rocks
And see the shepherds feed their flocks,
By shallow rivers, to whose falls
Melodious birds sing madrigals.

There will I make thee beds of roses
And a thousand fragrant posies,
A cap of flowers, and a kirtle
Embroider'd all with leaves of myrtle.

A gown made of the finest wool,
Which from our pretty lambs we pull,
Fair lined slippers for the cold,
With buckles of the purest gold.

A belt of straw and ivy buds,
With coral clasps and amber studs :
And if these pleasures may thee move,
Come live with me and be my Love.

Thy silver dishes for thy meat
As precious as the gods do eat,
Shall on an ivory table be
Prepared each day for thee and me.

The shepherd swains shall dance and sing
For thy delight each May-morning :
If these delights thy mind may move,
Come live with me and be my Love.

                              C. Marlowe

VIII

THE KITTEN AND FALLING LEAVES

SEE the Kitten on the wall,
    Sporting with the leaves that fall,
Withered leaves — one — two — and three —
From the lofty elder-tree !
Through the calm and frosty air
Of this morning bright and fair,
Eddying round and round they sink
Softly, slowly : one might think
From the motions that are made,
Every little leaf conveyed
Sylph or Fairy hither tending,
To this lower world descending,'
Each invisible and mute,
In his wavering parachute.
— But the Kitten, how she starts,
Crouches, stretches, paws, and darts !
First at one, and then its fellow,
Just as light, and just as yellow ;

There are many now — now one —
Now they stop and there are none :
What intenseness of desire
In her upward eye of fire !
With a tiger-leap half-way
Now she meets the coming prey,
Lets it go as fast, and then
Has it in her power again :
Now she works with three or four,
Like an Indian conjuror ;
Quick as he in feats of art,
Far beyond in joy of heart.
Were her antics played in the eye
Of a thousand standers-by,
Clapping hands with shouts and stare,
What would little Tabby care
For the plaudits of the crowd ?
Over happy to be proud,
Over wealthy in the treasure
Of her own exceeding pleasure !

W. Wordsworth

IX

THE FERRYMAN, VENUS, AND CUPID

AS I a fare had lately past,
And thought that side to ply,
I heard one, as it were, in haste,
A boat ! a boat ! to cry ;
Which as I was about to bring,
And came to view my fraught,
Thought I, what more than heavenly thing
Hath fortune hither brought ?

She, seeing mine eyes still on her were,
Soon, smilingly, quoth she,
Sirrah, look to your rudder there,
Why look'st thou thus at me?
And nimbly stepp'd into my boat
With her a little lad,
Naked and blind, yet did I note
That bow and shafts he had,
And two wings to his shoulders fixt,
Which stood like little sails,
With far more various colours mixt
Than be your peacocks' tails!
I seeing this little dapper elf
Such arms as these to bear,
Quoth I, thus softly to myself,
What strange things have we here?
I never saw the like, thought I,
'T is more than strange to me,
To have a child have wings to fly,
And yet want eyes to see.
Sure this is some devised toy,
Or it transform'd hath been,
For such a thing, half bird, half boy,
I think was never seen.
And in my boat I turn'd about,
And wistly view'd the lad,
And clearly I saw his eyes were out,
Though bow and shafts he had.
As wistly she did me behold,
How lik'st thou him? quoth she.
Why, well, quoth I, the better should,
Had he but eyes to see.
How say'st thou, honest friend, quoth she,
Wilt thou a 'prentice take?

I think, in time, though blind he be,
A ferryman he 'll make.
To guide my passage-boat, quoth I,
His fine hands were not made ;
He hath been bred too wantonly
To undertake my trade.
Why, help him to a master, then,
Quoth she, such youths be scant ;
It cannot be but there be men
That such a boy do want.
Quoth I, when you your best have done,
No better way you 'll find,
Than to a harper bind your son,
Since most of them are blind.
The lovely mother and the boy
Laugh'd heartily thereat,
As at some nimble jest or toy,
To hear my homely chat.
Quoth I, I pray you let me know,
Came he thus first to light,
Or by some sickness, hurt, or blow,
Deprived of his sight?
Nay, sure, quoth she, he thus was born.
'T is strange, born blind ! quoth I ;
I fear you put this as a scorn
On my simplicity.
Quoth she, thus blind I did him bear.
Quoth I, if 't be no lie,
Then he 's the first blind man, I 'll swear,
E'er practis'd archery.
A man ! quoth she, nay, there you miss,
He 's still a boy as now,
Nor to be elder than he is
The gods will him allow.

To be no elder than he is !
Then sure he is some sprite,
I straight reply'd.   Again at this
The goddess laugh'd outright.
It is a mystery to me,
An archer, and yet blind !
Quoth I again, how can it be,
That he his mark should find ?
The gods, quoth she, whose will it was
That he should want his sight,
That he in something should surpass
To recompense their spite,
Gave him this gift, though at his game
He still shot in the dark,
That he should have so certain aim,
As not to miss his mark.
By this time we were come ashore,
When me my fare she paid,
But not a word she utter'd more,
Nor had I her bewray'd.
Of Venus nor of Cupid I
Before did never hear,
But that a fisher coming by
Then told me who they were.

                              M. Drayton

X

SONG

UNDER the greenwood tree,
  Who loves to lie with me,
And tune his merry note
Unto the sweet bird's throat,
Come hither, come hither, come hither;
    Here shall he see
    No enemy
But winter and rough weather.

Who doth ambition shun,
And loves to live in the sun,
Seeking the food he eats,
And pleased with what he gets,
Come hither, come hither, come hither;
    Here shall he see
    No enemy
But winter and rough weather.

W. Shakespeare

XI

LUCY GRAY

Or Solitude

OFT I had heard of Lucy Gray:
  And, when I crossed the wild,
I chanced to see at break of day
The solitary child.

No mate, no comrade Lucy knew ;
She dwelt on a wide moor,
— The sweetest thing that ever grew
Beside a human door !

You yet may spy the fawn at play,
The hare upon the green ;
But the sweet face of Lucy Gray
Will never more be seen.

' To-night will be a stormy night —
You to the town must go ;
And take a lantern, child, to light
Your mother through the snow.'

' That, Father, will I gladly do !
'T is scarcely afternoon —
The minster-clock has just struck two,
And yonder is the moon !'

At this the Father raised his hook,
And snapped a fagot-band ;
He plied his work ; — and Lucy took
The lantern in her hand.

Not blither is the mountain roe :
With many a wanton stroke
Her feet disperse the powdery snow,
That rises up like smoke.

The storm came on before its time :
She wandered up and down ;
And many a hill did Lucy climb ;
But never reached the town.

The wretched parents all that night
Went shouting far and wide ;
But there was neither sound nor sight
To serve them for a guide.

At daybreak on a hill they stood
That overlooked the moor ;
And thence they saw the bridge of wood,
A furlong from their door.

They wept, and, turning homeward, cried,
' In heaven we all shall meet ! '
— When in the snow the mother spied
The print of Lucy's feet.

Then downward from the steep hill's edge
They tracked the footmarks small ;
And through the broken hawthorn hedge,
And by the long stone wall ;

And then an open field they crossed ;
The marks were still the same ;
They tracked them on, nor ever lost ;
And to the bridge they came.

They followed from the snowy bank
Those footmarks, one by one,
Into the middle of the plank ;
And further there were none !

— Yet some maintain that to this day
She is a living child ;
That you may see sweet Lucy Gray
Upon the lonesome wild.

O'er rough and smooth she trips along,
And never looks behind ;
And sings a solitary song
That whistles in the wind.
                    W. Wordsworth

XII

RAIN IN SUMMER

HOW beautiful is the rain !
     After the dust and the heat,
In the broad and fiery street,
In the narrow lane,
How beautiful is the rain !

How it clatters along the roofs,
Like the tramp of hoofs !
How it gushes and struggles out
From the throat of the overflowing spout !
Across the window-pane
It pours and pours ;
And swift and wide,
With a muddy tide,
Like a river down the gutter roars
The rain, the welcome rain !

The sick man from his chamber looks
At the twisted brooks ;
He can feel the cool
Breath of each little pool ;
His fevered brain
Grows calm again,
And he breathes a blessing on the rain.

From the neighbouring school
Come the boys,
With more than their wonted noise
And commotion ;
And down the wet streets
Sail their mimic fleets,
Till the treacherous pool
Engulfs them in its whirling
And turbulent ocean.

In the country on every side,
Where far and wide,
Like a leopard's tawny and spotted hide
Stretches the plain,
To the dry grass and the drier grain
How welcome is the rain !

In the furrowed land
The toilsome and patient oxen stand ;
Lifting the yoke-encumbered head,
With their dilated nostrils spread,
They silently inhale
The clover-scented gale,
And the vapours that arise
From the well-watered and smoking soil.
For this rest in the furrow after toil
Their large and lustrous eyes
Seem to thank the Lord,
More than man's spoken word.

Near at hand,
From under the sheltering trees,
The farmer sees
His pastures and his fields of grain,

2

As they bend their tops
To the numberless beating drops
Of the incessant rain.
He counts it as no sin
That he sees therein
Only his own thrift and gain.
      *   *   *   *H. W. Longfellow*

XIII

EPITAPH ON A HARE

HERE lies, whom hound did ne'er pursue,
   Nor swifter greyhound follow,
Whose foot ne'er tainted morning dew,
   Nor ear heard huntsman's hallo !

Old Tiney, surliest of his kind,
   Who, nurs'd with tender care,
And to domestic bounds confined,
   Was still a wild Jack-hare.

Though duly from my hand he took
   His pittance every night,
He did it with a jealous look,
   And, when he could, would bite.

His diet was of wheaten bread,
   And milk, and oats, and straw ;
Thistles, or lettuces instead,
   With sand to scour his maw.

On twigs of hawthorn he regaled,
   On pippin's russet peel,

And when his juicy salads failed,
   Sliced carrot pleased him well.

A Turkey carpet was his lawn,
   Whereon he loved to bound,
To skip and gambol like a fawn,
   And swing himself around.

His frisking was at evening hours,
   For then he lost his fear,
But most before approaching showers,
   Or when a storm drew near.

Eight years and five round-rolling moons
   He thus saw steal away,
Dozing out all his idle noons,
   And every night at play.

I kept him for his humours' sake,
   For he would oft beguile
My heart of thoughts that made it ache,
   And force me to a smile.

But now, beneath this walnut shade,
   He finds his long last home,
And waits, in snug concealment laid,
   Till gentler Puss shall come.

He, still more aged, feels the shocks
   From which no care can save,
And, partner once of Tiney's box,
   Must soon partake his grave.

                    W. Cowper

XIV

ABOU BEN ADHEM AND THE ANGEL

ABOU Ben Adhem (may his tribe increase)
　　Awoke one night from a deep dream of peace,
And saw within the moonlight in his room,
Making it rich, and like a lily in bloom,
An angel writing in a book of gold : —
Exceeding peace had made Ben Adhem bold,
And to the Presence in the room he said,
' What writest thou ? ' — The vision raised its head,
And, with a look made of all sweet accord,
Answer'd, ' The names of those who love the Lord.'
' And is mine one ? ' said Abou.　' Nay, not so,'
Replied the Angel.　Abou spoke more low,
But cheerly still ; and said, ' I pray thee then,
Write me as one that loves his fellow-men.'

The angel wrote and vanished.　The next night
It came again with a great wakening light,
And show'd the names whom love of God had bless'd,
And lo ! Ben Adhem's name led all the rest.

Leigh Hunt

XV

LA BELLE DAME SANS MERCY

AH, what can ail thee, wretched wight,
　　Alone and palely loitering ?
The sedge is wither'd from the lake,
　　And no birds sing.

Ah, what can ail thee, wretched wight,
   So haggard and so woe-begone?
The squirrel's granary is full,
   And the harvest's done.

I see a lily on thy brow,
   With anguish moist and fever dew;
And on thy cheek a fading rose
   Fast withereth too.

I met a Lady in the meads,
   Full beautiful, a fairy's child;
Her hair was long, her foot was light,
   And her eyes were wild.

I set her on my pacing steed,
   And nothing else saw all day long;
For sideways would she lean and sing
   A fairy's song.

I made a garland for her head,
   And bracelets too, and fragrant zone;
She look'd at me as she did love,
   And made sweet moan.

She found me roots of relish sweet,
   And honey wild, and manna dew;
And sure in language strange she said,
   I love thee true.

She took me to her elfin grot,
   And there she gazed and sighed deep,
And there I shut her wild sad eyes,
   So kissed to sleep.

And there we slumber'd on the moss,
And there I dream'd, ah, woe betide,
The latest dream I ever dream'd
On the cold hill-side.

I saw pale kings, and princes too,
Pale warriors, death-pale were they all ;
Who cried, ' La belle Dame sans mercy
Hath thee in thrall ! '

I saw their starved lips in the gloom
With horrid warning gaped wide,
And I awoke and found me here,
On the cold hill-side.

And this is why I sojourn here
Alone and palely loitering,
Though the sedge is wither'd from the lake,
And no birds sing.

J. Keats

XVI

WINTER

WHEN icicles hang by the wall,
And Dick the Shepherd blows his nail,
And Tom bears logs into the hall,
And milk comes frozen home in pail ;
When blood is nipt, and ways be foul,
Then nightly sings the staring owl
Tuwhoo !
Tuwhit ! tuwhoo !   A merry note
While greasy Joan doth keel the pot.

When all around the wind doth blow,
   And coughing drowns the parson's saw,
And birds sit brooding in the snow,
   And Marian's nose looks red and raw,
When roasted crabs hiss in the bowl,
Then nightly sings the staring owl
                Tuwhoo !
Tuwhit ! tuwhoo !   A merry note
While greasy Joan doth keel the pot.
              W. Shakespeare

XVII

THE INCHCAPE ROCK

NO stir in the air, no stir in the sea,
   The ship was as still as she could be,
Her sails from heaven received no motion,
Her keel was steady in the ocean.

Without either sign or sound of their shock
The waves flow'd over the Inchcape Rock ;
So little they rose, so little they fell,
They did not move the Inchcape Bell.

The good old Abbot of Aberbrothok
Had placed that bell on the Inchcape Rock ;
On a buoy in the storm it floated and swung,
And over the waves its warning rung.

When the Rock was hid by the surges' swell,
The Mariners heard the warning bell ;
And then they knew the perilous Rock,
And blest the Abbot of Aberbrothok.

The sun in heaven was shining gay,
All things were joyful on that day ;
The sea-birds scream'd as they wheel'd round,
And there was joyance in their sound.

The buoy of the Inchcape Bell was seen
A darker speck on the ocean green ;
Sir Ralph the Rover walk'd his deck,
And he fix'd his eye on a darker speck.

He felt the cheering power of spring,
It made him whistle, it made him sing ;
His heart was mirthful to excess,
But the Rover's mirth was wickedness.

His eye was on the Inchcape float ;
Quoth he, ' My men, put out the boat,
And row me to the Inchcape Rock,
And I 'll plague the priest of Aberbrothok.'

The boat is lower'd, the boatmen row,
And to the Inchcape Rock they go ;
Sir Ralph bent over from the boat,
And he cut the bell from the Inchcape float.

Down sunk the bell, with a gurgling sound,
The bubbles rose and burst around ;
Quoth Sir Ralph, ' The next who comes to the Rock
Won't bless the Abbot of Aberbrothok.'

Sir Ralph the Rover sail'd away,
He scour'd the seas for many a day ;
And now grown rich with plunder'd store,
He steers his course for Scotland's shore.

So thick a haze o'erspreads the sky
They cannot see the sun on high;
The wind hath blown a gale all day,
At evening it hath died away.

On the deck the Rover takes his stand,
So dark it is they see no land.
Quoth Sir Ralph, 'It will be lighter soon,
For there is the dawn of the rising moon.'

'Canst hear,' said one, 'the breakers roar?
For methinks we should be near the shore;
Now where we are I cannot tell,
But I wish I could hear the Inchcape Bell.'

They hear no sound, the swell is strong;
Though the wind hath fallen, they drift along,
Till the vessel strikes with a shivering shock:
Cried they, 'It is the Inchcape Rock!'

Sir Ralph the Rover tore his hair,
He curst himself in his despair;
The waves rush in on every side,
The ship is sinking beneath the tide.

But even in his dying fear
One dreadful sound could the Rover hear,
A sound as if with the Inchcape Bell
The fiends below were ringing his knell.

R. Southey

XVIII

WRITTEN IN MARCH

THE cock is crowing,
   The stream is flowing,
The small birds twitter,
The lake doth glitter,
The green field sleeps in the sun ;
   The oldest and youngest
   Are at work with the strongest ;
   The cattle are grazing,
   Their heads never raising ;
There are forty feeding like one !

   Like an army defeated
   The snow hath retreated,
   And now doth fare ill
   On the top of the bare hill ;
The Plough-boy is whooping anon, anon.
   There 's joy in the mountains ;
   There 's life in the fountains ;
   Small clouds are sailing,
   Blue sky prevailing ;
The rain is over and gone !

                W. Wordsworth

XIX

LORD RANDAL

O WHERE have ye been, Lord Randal, my son?
O where have ye been, my handsome young
man?'
'I have been to the wood; mother, make my bed
soon,
For I'm weary with hunting, and fain would lie down.'

'Where got ye your dinner, Lord Randal, my son?
Where got ye your dinner, my handsome young man?'
'I dined with my love; mother, make my bed soon,
For I'm weary with hunting, and fain would lie down.'

'What got ye to dinner, Lord Randal, my son?
What got ye to dinner, my handsome young man?'
'I got eels boil'd in broth; mother, make my bed soon,
For I'm weary with hunting, and fain would lie down.'

'And where are your bloodhounds, Lord Randal, my
son?
And where are your bloodhounds, my handsome young
man?'
'O, they swell'd and they died; mother, make my bed
soon,
For I'm weary with hunting, and fain would lie down.'

'O, I fear ye are poison'd, Lord Randal, my son!
O, I fear ye are poison'd, my handsome young man!'
'O, yes, I am poison'd! mother, make my bed soon,
For I'm sick at the heart, and I fain would lie down.'
                              Old Ballad

XX

JOHN BARLEYCORN

THERE was three kings into the East,
    Three kings both great and high,
And they hae sworn a solemn oath
    John Barleycorn should die.

They took a plough and ploughed him down,
    Put clods upon his head,
And they hae sworn a solemn oath,
    John Barleycorn was dead.

But the cheerful spring came kindly on,
    And showers began to fall ;
John Barleycorn got up again,
    And sore surprised them all.

The sultry suns of summer came,
    And he grew thick and strong,
His head well armed wi' pointed spears,
    That no one should him wrong.

The sober autumn entered mild,
    When he grew wan and pale ;
His bending joints and drooping head
    Show'd he began to fail.

His colour sickened more and more,
    He faded into age ;
And then his enemies began
    To show their deadly rage.

They 've ta'en a weapon long and sharp,
 And cut him by the knee ;
And tied him fast upon the cart,
 Like a rogue for forgerie.

They laid him down upon his back,
 And cudgell'd him full sore ;
They hung him up before the storm,
 And turn'd him o'er and o'er.

They filled up a darksome pit
 With water to the brim,
They heaved in John Barleycorn,
 There let him sink or swim.

They laid him out upon the floor,
 To work him further woe,
And still, as signs of life appear'd,
 They toss'd him to and fro.

They wasted, o'er a scorching flame,
 The marrow of his bones ;
But a miller used him worst of all,
 For he crush'd him between two stones.

And they hae ta'en his very heart's blood,
 And drank it round and round ;
And still the more and more they drank,
 Their joy did more abound.

John Barleycorn was a hero bold,
 Of noble enterprise ;
For if you do but taste his blood,
 'T will make your courage rise.

Then let us toast John Barleycorn,
  Each man a glass in hand ;
And may his great posterity
  Ne'er fail in old Scotland !

Old Ballad

XXI

MARY–ANN'S CHILD

MARY-ANN was alone with her baby in arms,
  In her house with the trees overhead,
For her husband was out in the night and the storms,
  In his business a-toiling for bread ;
And she, as the wind in the elm-heads did roar,
Did grieve to think he was all night out of door.

And her kinsfolk and neighbours did say of her child
  (Under the lofty elm-tree),
That a prettier never did babble and smile
  Up a-top of a proud mother's knee ;
And his mother did toss him, and kiss him, and call
Him her darling, and life, and her hope and her all.

But she found in the evening the child was not well
  (Under the gloomy elm-tree),
And she felt she could give all the world for to tell
  Of a truth what his ailing could be ;
And she thought on him last in her prayers at night,
And she look'd at him last as she put out the light.

And she found him grow worse in the dead of the night
  (Under the gloomy elm-tree),

And she press'd him against her warm bosom so tight,
    And she rock'd him so sorrowfully ;
And there, in his anguish, a-nestling he lay,
Till his struggles grew weak, and his cries died away.

And the moon was a-shining down into the place
    (Under the gloomy elm-tree),
And his mother could see that his lips and his face
    Were as white as clean ashes could be ;
And her tongue was a-tied, and her still heart did swell
Till her senses came back with the first tear that fell.

Never more can she feel his warm face in her breast
    (Under the leafy elm-tree),
For his eyes are a-shut, and his hands are at rest,
    And he 's now from his pain a-set free ;
For his soul we do know is to heaven a-fled,
Where no pain is a-known, and no tears are a-shed.

W. Barnes

XXII

THE USEFUL PLOUGH

A COUNTRY life is sweet !
    In moderate cold and heat,
    To walk in the air, how pleasant and fair,
In every field of wheat,
    The fairest of flowers adorning the bowers,
And every meadow's brow ;
    So that I say, no courtier may
    Compare with them who clothe in gray,
And follow the useful plough.

They rise with the morning lark,
And labour till almost dark ;
    Then folding their sheep, they hasten to sleep ;
While every pleasant park
    Next morning is ringing with birds that are singing,
On each green, tender bough.
    With what content and merriment,
Their days are spent, whose minds are bent
    To follow the useful plough !

Old Song

XXIII

A WREN'S NEST

AMONG the dwellings framed by birds
    In field or forest with nice care,
Is none that with the little wren's
    In snugness may compare.

No door the tenement requires,
    And seldom needs a laboured roof ;
Yet is it to the fiercest sun
    Impervious, and storm-proof.

So warm, so beautiful withal,
    In perfect fitness for its aim,
That to the Kind, by special grace,
    Their instinct surely came.

And when for their abodes they seek
    An opportune recess,
The hermit has no finer eye
    For shadowy quietness.

These find, 'mid ivied abbey walls,
  A canopy in some still nook ;
Others are pent-housed by a brae
  That overhangs a brook.

There to the brooding bird her mate
  Warbles by fits his low clear song ;
And by the busy streamlet both
  Are sung to all day long.

Or in sequestered lanes they build,
  Where, till the flitting bird's return,
Her eggs within the nest repose,
  Like relics in an urn.

But still, where general choice is good,
  There is a better and a best ;
And, among fairest objects, some
  Are fairer than the rest.

This, one of those small builders proved
  In a green covert, where from out
The forehead of a pollard oak
  The leafy antlers sprout ;

For she who planned the mossy lodge,
  Mistrusting her evasive skill,
Had to a primrose looked for aid,
  Her wishes to fulfil.

High on the trunk's projecting brow,
  And fixed an infant's span above
The budding flowers, peeped forth the nest,
  The prettiest of the grove !

3

The treasure proudly did I show
  To some whose minds without disdain
Can turn to little things ; but once
  Looked up for it in vain :

'T is gone — a ruthless spoiler's prey,
  Who heeds not beauty, love, or song,
'T is gone ! (so seemed it,) and we grieved,
  Indignant at the wrong.

Just three days after, passing by
  In clearer light, the moss-built cell
I saw, espied its shaded mouth ;
  And felt that all was well.

The primrose for a veil had spread
  The largest of her upright leaves ;
And thus, for purposes benign,
  A simple flower deceives.

Concealed from friends who might disturb
  Thy quiet with no ill intent,
Secure from evil eyes and hands
  On barbarous plunder bent,

Rest, mother-bird ! and when thy young
  Take flight, and thou art free to roam,
When withered is the guardian flower,
  And empty thy late home,

Think how ye prospered, thou and thine,
  Amid the unviolated grove,
Housed near the growing primrose tuft
  In foresight, or in love.

                              W. Wordsworth

XXIV

A FINE DAY

CLEAR had the day been from the dawn,
  All chequer'd was the sky,
Thin clouds like scarfs of cobweb lawn
Veil'd heaven's most glorious eye.
The wind had no more strength than this,
That leisurely it blew,
To make one leaf the next to kiss
That closely by it grew.

M. Drayton

XXV

CASABIANCA

A True Story

THE boy stood on the burning deck
  Whence all but he had fled ;
The flame that lit the battle's wreck
  Shone round him o'er the dead.

The flames roll'd on.   He would not go
  Without his father's word ;
That father faint in death below,
  His voice no longer heard.

He called aloud : ' Say, father, say
  If yet my task is done ! '
He knew not that the chieftain lay
  Unconscious of his son.

'Speak, father!' once again he cried,
　'If I may yet be gone!'
And but the booming shots replied,
　And fast the flames roll'd on.

Upon his brow he felt their breath,
　And in his waving hair,
And look'd from that lone post of death
　In still, yet brave despair;

And shouted but once more aloud,
　'My father! must I stay?'
While o'er him fast through sail and shroud,
　The wreathing fires made way.

They wrapt the ship in splendour wild,
　They caught the flag on high,
And streamed above the gallant child
　Like banners in the sky.

Then came a burst of thunder-sound —
　The boy — oh! where was he?
Ask of the winds that far around
　With fragments strewed the sea,

With mast, and helm, and pennon fair,
　That well had borne their part;
But the noblest thing that perished there
　Was that young faithful heart!

F. Hemans

XXVI

SIGNS OF RAIN

THE hollow winds begin to blow,
   The clouds look black, the glass is low,
The soot falls down, the spaniels sleep,
The spiders from their cobwebs peep :
Last night the sun went pale to bed,
The moon in halos hid her head ;
The boding shepherd heaves a sigh,
For, see, a rainbow spans the sky :
The walls are damp, the ditches smell,
Closed is the pink-eyed pimpernel.
Hark how the chairs and tables crack !
Old Betty's joints are on the rack ;
Loud quack the ducks, the peacocks cry,
The distant hills are seeming nigh.
How restless are the snorting swine ;
The busy flies disturb the kine ;
Low o'er the grass the swallow wings,
The cricket too, how sharp he sings ;
Puss on the hearth, with velvet paws,
Sits wiping o'er her whiskered jaws.
Through the clear stream the fishes rise,
And nimbly catch the incautious flies.
The glow-worms, numerous and bright,
Illumed the dewy dell last night.
At dusk the squalid toad was seen,
Hopping and crawling o'er the green ;
The whirling wind the dust obeys,
And in the rapid eddy plays ;
The frog has changed his yellow vest,
And in a russet coat is dressed.

Though June, the air is cold and still,
The mellow blackbird's voice is shrill.
My dog, so altered in his taste,
Quits mutton-bones on grass to feast ;
And see yon rooks, how odd their flight,
They imitate the gliding kite,
And seem precipitate to fall,
As if they felt the piercing ball.
'T will surely rain, I see with sorrow,
Our jaunt must be put off to-morrow.

E. Jenner

XXVII

HOW THEY BROUGHT THE GOOD NEWS FROM GHENT TO AIX

I SPRANG to the stirrup, and Joris, and he ;
I galloped, Dirck galloped, we galloped all three ;
'Good speed !' cried the watch, as the gate-bolts un-
        drew ;
'Speed !' echoed the wall to us galloping through ;
Behind shut the postern, the lights sank to rest,
And into the midnight we galloped abreast.

Not a word to each other ; we kept the great pace
Neck by neck, stride by stride, never changing our
        place ;
I turned in my saddle and made its girths tight,
Then shortened each stirrup, and set the pique right,
Rebuckled the cheek-strap, chained slacker the bit,
Nor galloped less steadily Roland a whit.

'T was moonset at starting ; but, while we drew near
Lokeren, the cocks crew and twilight dawned clear ;
At Boom, a great yellow star came out to see ;
At Düffeld, 't was morning as plain as could be ;
And from Mecheln church-steeple we heard the half-
     chime,
So Joris broke silence with, ' Yet there is time ! '

At Aerschot, up leaped of a sudden the sun,
And against him the cattle stood black every one,
To stare through the mist at us galloping past,
And I saw my stout galloper, Roland, at last,
With resolute shoulders each butting away
The haze, as some bluff river headland its spray ;

And his low head and crest, just one sharp ear bent back
For my voice, and the other pricked out on his track ;
And one eye's black intelligence, — ever that glance
O'er its white edge at me, his own master, askance !
And the thick heavy spume-flakes which aye and anon
His fierce lips shook upwards in galloping on.

By Hasselt, Dirck groaned ; and cried Joris, ' Stay
     spur !
Your Roos galloped bravely, the fault 's not in her,
We 'll remember at Aix ' — for one heard the quick
     wheeze
Of her chest, saw the stretched neck, and staggering
     knees,
And sunk tail, and horrible heave of the flank,
As down on her haunches she shuddered and sank.

So we were left galloping, Joris and I,
Past Loos and past Tongres, no cloud in the sky ;

The broad sun above laughed a pitiless laugh,
'Neath our foot broke the brittle bright stubble like
  chaff;
Till over by Dalhem a dome-tower sprang white,
And 'Gallop,' cried Joris, 'for Aix is in sight!'

'How they'll greet us!' and all in a moment his roan
Rolled neck and croup over, lay dead as a stone;
And there was my Roland to bear the whole weight
Of the news which alone could save Aix from her fate,
With his nostrils like pits full of blood to the brim,
And with circles of red for his eye-sockets' rim.

Then I cast my loose buff-coat, each holster let fall,
Shook off both my jack-boots, let go belt and all,
Stood up in the stirrup, leaned, patted his ear,
Called my Roland his pet name, my horse without peer;
Clapped my hands, laughed and sang, any noise, bad
  or good,
Till at length into Aix Roland galloped and stood.

And all I remember is friends flocking round
As I sate with his head 'twixt my knees on the ground,
And no voice but was praising this Roland of mine,
As I poured down his throat our last measure of wine,
Which (the burgesses voted by common consent)
Was no more than his due who brought good news from
  Ghent.

         R. Browning

XXVIII

THE RAINBOW

A FRAGMENT of a rainbow bright
　　Through the moist air I see,
All dark and damp on yonder height,
　　All bright and clear to me.

An hour ago the storm was here,
　　The gleam was far behind,
So will our joys and grief appear,
　　When earth has ceased to blind.

Grief will be joy if on its edge
　　Fall soft that holiest ray,
Joy will be grief if no faint pledge
　　Be there of heavenly day.
　　　　　　　　　　J. Keble

XXIX

THE RAVEN AND THE OAK

UNDERNEATH an old oak tree
　　There was of swine a huge company,
That grunted as they crunch'd the mast :
For that was ripe and fell full last.
Then they trotted away, for the wind it grew high :
One acorn they left and no more might you spy.
Next came a Raven that liked not such folly :
He belonged, they did say, to the witch Melancholy !

Blacker was he than blackest jet,
Flew low in the rain and his feathers not wet.
He picked up the acorn and buried it straight
By the side of a river both deep and great.
      Where then did the Raven go?
      He went high and low,
  Over hill, over dale, did the black Raven go.
      Many autumns, many springs
      Travelled he with wandering wings:
      Many summers, many winters —
      I can't tell half his adventures.

At length he came back, and with him a she,
And the acorn was grown to a tall oak tree.
They built them a nest in the topmost bough,
And young ones they had and were happy enow.
But soon came a woodman in leathern guise,
His brow, like a pent-house, hung over his eyes.
He'd an axe in his hand, not a word he spoke,
But with many a hem! and a sturdy stroke,
At length he brought down the poor Raven's old oak.
His young ones were killed, for they could not depart,
And their mother did die of a broken heart.
The boughs from the trunk the woodman did sever;
And they floated it down on the course of the river.
They sawed it in planks, and its bark they did strip,
And with this tree and others they made a good ship.
The ship it was launched; but in sight of the land
Such a storm there did rise as no ship could withstand.
It bulged on a rock, and the waves rushed in fast:
Round and round flew the Raven and cawed to the
      blast.
He heard the last shriek of the perishing souls —
See! see! o'er the top-mast the mad water rolls!

Right glad was the Raven, and off he went fleet,
And Death riding home on a cloud he did meet,
And he thanked him again and again for this treat :
    They had taken his all, and revenge it was sweet.
                    S. T. Coleridge

XXX

ODE TO THE CUCKOO

HAIL, beauteous stranger of the grove !
    Thou messenger of spring !
Now Heaven repairs thy rural seat,
    And woods thy welcome sing.

What time the daisy decks the green,
    Thy certain voice we hear ;
Hast thou a star to guide thy path,
    Or mark the rolling year ?

Delightful visitant, with thee
    I hail the time of flowers,
And hear the sound of music sweet
    From birds among the bowers.

The school-boy wandering through the wood
    To pull the primrose gay,
Starts the new voice of spring to hear,
    And imitates the lay.

What time the pea puts on the bloom
    Thou fliest thy vocal vale,
An annual guest in other lands,
    Another spring to hail.

Sweet bird ! thy bower is ever green,
　Thy sky is ever clear ;
Thou hast no sorrow in thy song,
　No winter in thy year !

O could I fly, I 'd fly with thee !
　We 'd make, with joyful wing,
Our annual visit o'er the globe,
　Companions of the spring.
　　　　　　　　　J. Logan

XXXI

ROBIN HOOD AND ALLIN A DALE

COME listen to me, you gallants so free,
　All you that love mirth for to hear,
And I will tell you of a bold outlaw
　That lived in Nottinghamshire.

As Robin Hood in the forest stood,
　All under the greenwood tree,
There he was aware of a brave young man
　As fine as fine might be.

The youngster was cloth'd in scarlet red,
　In scarlet fine and gay ;
And he did frisk it over the plain,
　And chanted a roundelay.

As Robin Hood next morning stood
　Amongst the leaves so gay ;
There did he espy the same young man,
　Come drooping along the way.

The scarlet he wore the day before
　　It was clean cast away ;
And at every step he fetch'd a sigh,
　　' Alack and a well-a-day ! '

Then stepp'd forth brave Little John,
　　And Midge, the miller's son,
Which made the young man bend his bow,
　　Whon as he saw them come.

'Stand off, stand off ! ' the young man said,
　　' What is your will with me ? '
'You must come before our master straight,
　　Under yon greenwood tree.'

And when he came bold Robin before,
　　Robin asked him courteously,
'O, hast thou any money to spare
　　For my merry men and me ? '

'I have no money,' the young man said,
　　' But five shillings and a ring ;
And that I have kept this seven long years,
　　To have it at my wedding.

' Yesterday I should have married a maid,
　　But she soon from me was tane,
And chosen to be an old knight's delight,
　　Whereby my poor heart is slain.'

' What is thy name ? ' then said Robin Hood,
　　' Come tell me without any fail ' :
'By the faith of my body,' then said the young man,
　　' My name it is Allin a Dale.'

'What wilt thou give me?' said Robin Hood,
  'In ready gold or fee,
To help thee to thy true love again,
  And deliver her unto thee?'

'I have no money,' then quoth the young man,
  'No ready gold nor fee,
But I will swear upon a book
  Thy true servant for to be.'

'How many miles is it to thy true love?
  Come tell me without guile':
'By the faith of my body,' then said the young man,
  'It is but five little mile.'

Then Robin he hasted over the plain,
  He did neither stint nor lin,
Until he came unto the church,
  Where Allin should keep his wedding.

'What hast thou here?' the bishop then said,
  'I prithee now tell unto me':
'I am a bold harper,' quoth Robin Hood,
  'And the best in the north country.'

'O welcome, O welcome,' the bishop he said,
  'That music best pleaseth me';
'You shall have no music,' quoth Robin Hood,
  'Till the bride and the bridegroom I see.'

With that came in a wealthy knight,
  Which was both grave and old,
And after him a finikin lass,
  Did shine like the glistering gold.

'This is not a fit match,' quoth bold Robin Hood,
　'That you do seem to make here,
For since we are come into the church,
　The bride shall choose her own dear.'

Then Robin Hood put his horn to his mouth,
　And blew blasts two or three ;
When four-and-twenty bowmen bold
　Came leaping over the lea.

And when they came into the churchyard,
　Marching all on a row,
The very first man was Allin a Dale,
　To give bold Robin his bow.

'This is thy true love,' Robin he said,
　'Young Allin as I hear say ;
And you shall be married at this same time,
　Before we depart away.'

'That shall not be,' the bishop he said,
　'For thy word shall not stand ;
They shall be three times asked in the church,
　As the law is of our land.'

Robin Hood pulled off the bishop's coat,
　And put it upon Little John ;
'By the faith of my body,' then Robin said,
　'This cloth doth make thee a man.'

When Little John went into the quire ;
　The people began to laugh ;
He asked them seven times in the church,
　Lest three times should not be enough.

'Who gives me this maid?' said Little John;
   Quoth Robin Hood, 'That do I,
And he that takes her from Allin a Dale,
   Full dearly he shall her buy.'

And thus having end of this merry wedding,
   The bride looked like a queen;
And so they returned to the merry greenwood,
   Amongst the leaves so green.

Old Ballad

XXXII

VIOLETS

UNDER the green hedges after the snow,
   There do the dear little violets grow,
Hiding their modest and beautiful heads
Under the hawthorn in soft mossy beds.

Sweet as the roses, and blue as the sky,
Down there do the dear little violets lie;
Hiding their heads where they scarce may be seen,
By the leaves you may know where the violet hath
   been.

J. Moultrie

XXXIII

THE PALMER

' OPEN the door, some pity to show !
   Keen blows the northern wind !
The glen is white with the drifted snow,
   And the path is hard to find.

  No outlaw seeks your castle gate,
   From chasing the king's deer,
Though even an outlaw's wretched state
   Might claim compassion here.

' A weary Palmer worn and weak,
   I wander from my sin ;
O, open, for Our Lady's sake !
   A pilgrim's blessing win !

' The hare is crouching in her form,
   The hart beside the hind ;
An aged man, amid the storm,
   No shelter can I find.

' You hear the Ettrick's sullen roar,
   Dark, deep, and strong is he,
And I must ford the Ettrick o'er,
   Unless you pity me.

' The iron gate is bolted hard,
   At which I knock in vain ;
The owner's heart is closer barr'd,
   Who hears me thus complain.

    4

'Farewell, farewell! and Heaven grant,
　　When old and frail you be,
You never may the shelter want,
　　That's now denied to me!'

The Ranger on his couch lay warm,
　　And heard him plead in vain;
But oft, amid December's storm,
　　He'll hear that voice again:

For lo, when through the vapours dank
　　Morn shone on Ettrick fair,
A corpse, amid the alders rank,
　　A Palmer welter'd there.

　　　　　　　　　　Sir W. Scott

XXXIV

THE FORSAKEN MERMAN

COME, dear children, let us away;
　　Down and away below.
Now my brothers call from the bay;
Now the great winds shorewards blow;
Now the salt tides seawards flow;
Now the wild white horses play,
Champ and chafe and toss in the spray.
　　Children dear, let us away.
　　　　This way, this way.

Call her once before you go.
　　Call once yet,
In a voice that she will know:
　　'Margaret! Margaret!'

Children's voices should be dear
(Call once more) to a mother's ear :
Children's voices wild with pain.
  Surely she will come again.
Call her once, and come away.
   This way, this way,
'Mother dear, we cannot stay.'
The wild white horses foam and fret,
  Margaret ! Margaret !

Come, dear children, come away down.
   Call no more.
One last look at the white-walled town,
And the little gray church on the windy shore,
   Then come down.
She will not come though you call all day.
   Come away, come away.

Children dear, was it yesterday
We heard the sweet bells over the bay?
  In the caverns where we lay,
  Through the surf and through the swell,
The far-off sound of a silver bell ?
Sand-strewn caverns cool and deep,
Where the winds are all asleep ;
Where the spent lights quiver and gleam ;
Where the salt weed sways in the stream ;
Where the sea-beasts rang'd all round
Feed in the ooze of their pasture ground ;
Where the sea-snakes coil and twine,
Dry their mail and bask in the brine ;
Where great whales come sailing by,
Sail and sail, with unshut eye,
Round the world for ever and aye ?

When did music come this way?
Children dear, was it yesterday?

Children dear, was it yesterday
(Call yet once) that she went away?
Once she sat with you and me,
On a red gold throne in the heart of the sea.
And the youngest sat on her knee.
She comb'd its bright hair, and she tended it well,
When down swung the sound of the far-off bell,
She sigh'd, she look'd up through the clear green
sea,
She said, 'I must go, for my kinsfolk pray
In the little gray church on the shore to-day.
'T will be Easter-time in the world — ah me!
And I lose my poor soul, Merman, here with thee.'
I said : 'Go up, dear heart, through the waves :
Say thy prayer, and come back to the kind sea-
caves.'
She smiled, she went up through the surf in the bay,
Children dear, was it yesterday?

Children dear, were we long alone?
' The sea grows stormy, the little ones moan ;
Long prayers,' I said, 'in the world they say.'
'Come,' I said, and we rose through the surf in the
bay.
We went up the beach in the sandy down   •
Where the sea-stocks bloom, to the white-walled town,
Through the narrow paved streets, where all was still,
To the little gray church on the windy hill.
From the church came a murmur of folk at their
prayers,
But we stood without in the cold blowing airs.

We climb'd on the graves on the stones worn with rains,
And we gazed up the aisle through the small leaded
      panes,
   She sat by the pillar; we saw her clear;
   'Margaret, hist! come quick, we are here.
   Dear heart,' I said, 'we are here alone.
   The sea grows stormy, the little ones moan.'
But, ah, she gave me never a look,
For her eyes were seal'd to the holy book.
   'Loud prays the priest; shut stands the door.'
Come away, children, call no more,
Come away, come down, call no more.

   Down, down, down,
   Down to the depths of the sea.
She sits at her wheel in the humming town,
      Singing most joyfully.
Hark what she sings: 'O joy, O joy,
From the humming street, and the child with its toy,
From the priest and the bell, and the holy well,
   From the wheel where I spun,
   And the blessed light of the sun.'
   And so she sings her fill,
   Singing most joyfully,
   Till the shuttle falls from her hand,
   And the whizzing wheel stands still.
She steals to the window and looks at the sand;
   And over the sand at the sea;
   And her eyes are set in a stare;
   And anon there breaks a sigh,
   And anon there drops a tear,
   From a sorrow-clouded eye,
   And a heart sorrow-laden,
      A long, long sigh,

For the cold strange eyes of a little Mermaiden,
And the gleam of her golden hair.

Come away, away, children,
Come, children, come down.
The hoarse wind blows colder,
Lights shine in the town.
She will start from her slumber
When gusts shake the door ;
She will hear the winds howling,
Will hear the waves roar.
We shall see, while above us
The waves roar and whirl,
A ceiling of amber,
A pavement of pearl.
Singing, ' Here came a mortal,
But faithless was she,
And alone dwell forever
The kings of the sea.'

But, children, at midnight,
When soft the winds blow,
When clear falls the moonlight,
When spring-tides are low ;
When sweet airs come seaward
From heaths starr'd with broom ;
And high rocks throw mildly
On the blanch'd sands a gloom :
Up the still, glistening beaches,
Up the creeks we will hie ;
Over banks of bright seaweed
The ebb-tide leaves dry.
We will gaze from the sand-hills,
At the white sleeping town ;

At the church on the hill-side —
    And then come back, down.
Singing, ' There dwells a loved one,
But cruel is she :
She left lonely forever
The kings of the sea.'
        M. Arnold

XXXV

THE SANDS O' DEE

I

' O MARY, go and call the cattle home,
    And call the cattle home,
    And call the cattle home,
  Across the sands o' Dee ! '
The western wind was wild and dank with foam,
    And all alone went she.

2

The creeping tide came up along the sand,
    And o'er and o'er the sand,
    And round and round the sand,
  As far as eye could see ;
The blinding mist came down and hid the land —
    And never home came she.

3

Oh, is it weed, or fish, or floating hair ? —
    A tress o' golden hair,
    O' drowned maiden's hair,
  Above the nets at sea.

Was never salmon yet that shone so fair
  Among the stakes on Dee.

4

They row'd her in across the rolling foam,
  The cruel crawling foam,
  The cruel hungry foam,
 To her grave beside the sea :
But still the boatmen hear her call the cattle home,
  Across the sands o' Dee.

                C. Kingsley

XXXVI

THE LOSS OF THE ROYAL GEORGE

TOLL for the brave !
  The brave that are no more !
All sunk beneath the wave,
  Fast by their native shore !

Eight hundred of the brave,
  Whose courage well was tried,
Had made the vessel heel,
  And laid her on her side.

A land breeze shook the shrouds,
  And she was overset ;
Down went the Royal George,
  With all her crew complete.

Toll for the brave !
  Brave Kempenfelt is gone ;
His last sea-fight is fought,
  His work of glory done.

It was not in the battle ;
  No tempest gave the shock :
She sprang no fatal leak ;
  She ran upon no rock.

His sword was in its sheath,
  His fingers held the pen,
When Kempenfelt went down,
  With twice four hundred men.

Weigh the vessel up,
  Once dreaded by our foes !
And mingle with our cup
  The tear that England owes.

Her timbers yet are sound,
  And she may float again,
Full charged with England's thunder,
  And plough the distant main.

But Kempenfelt is gone,
  His victories are o'er ;
And he and his eight hundred
  Shall plough the waves no more.

W. Cowper

XXXVII

A SEA DIRGE

FULL fathom five thy father lies :
　　Of his bones are coral made :
Those are pearls that were his eyes ;
　　Nothing of him that doth fade,
But doth suffer a sea change
Into something rich and strange ;
Sea-nymphs hourly ring his knell :
Hark ! now I hear them, —
　　　　Ding, dong, bell.

W. Shakespeare

XXXVIII

THE ANCIENT MARINER

IT is an ancient Mariner,
　　And he stoppeth one of three.
" By thy long gray beard and glittering eye,
Now wherefore stopp'st thou me ?

" The Bridegroom's doors are open'd wide,
And I am next of kin :
The guests are met, the feast is set :
May'st hear the merry din."

He holds him with his glittering eye —
The Wedding-Guest stood still,
And listens like a three years' child :
The Mariner hath his will.

The Wedding-Guest sat on a stone :
He cannot choose but hear ;
And thus spake on that ancient man,
The bright-eyed Mariner.

" The ship was cheered, the harbour cleared,"
Merrily did we drop
Below the kirk, below the hill,
Below the lighthouse top.

" The sun came up upon the left,
Out of the sea came he,
And he shone bright, and on the right
Went down into the sea.

" Higher and higher every day,
Till over the mast at noon " —
The Wedding-Guest here beat his breast,
For he heard the loud bassoon.

The Bride hath paced into the hall :
Red as a rose is she ;
Nodding their heads before her goes
The merry minstrelsy.

The Wedding-Guest he beat his breast,
Yet he cannot choose but hear ;
And thus spake on that ancient man,
The bright-eyed Mariner.

" And now the storm-blast came, and he
Was tyrannous and strong :
He struck with his o'ertaking wings,
And chased us south along.

" With sloping masts and dipping prow,
As who pursued with yell and blow
Still treads the shadow of his foe,
And forward bends his head,
The ship drove fast, loud roared the blast,
And southward aye we fled.

"And now there came both mist and snow,
And it grew wondrous cold :
And ice, mast-high, came floating by,
As green as emerald.

" And through the drifts the snowy clifts
Did send a dismal sheen :
Nor shapes of men nor beasts we ken —
The ice was all between.

" The ice was here, the ice was there,
The ice was all around :
It cracked and growled, and roared and howled,
Like noises in a swound !

" At length did cross an Albatross,
Thorough the fog it came ;
As if it had been a Christian soul,
We hailed it in God's name.

"It ate the food it ne'er had eat,
And round and round it flew,
The ice did split with a thunder-fit ;
The helmsman steered us through !

" And a good south wind sprung up behind ;
The Albatross did follow,

And every day, for food or play,
Came to the mariner's hollo !

" In mist or cloud, on mast or shroud,
It perched for vespers nine ;
Whiles all the night, through fog-smoke white,
Glimmered the white moonshine."

" God save thee, ancient Mariner !
From the fiends that plague thee thus ! —
Why look'st thou so ? "   " With my cross-bow
I shot the Albatross.

" And I had done a hellish thing,
And it would work 'em woe :
For all averr'd I had killed the bird
That made the breeze to blow !
' Ah wretch ! ' said they, ' the bird to slay,
That made the wind to blow ! '

" Nor dim nor red, like God's own head,
The glorious Sun uprist :
Then all averred, I had killed the bird
That brought the fog and mist.
'T was right, said they, such birds to slay,
That bring the fog and mist.

" Down dropt the breeze, the sails dropt down,
'T was sad as sad could be ;
And we did speak only to break
The silence of the sea.

" Day after day, day after day,
We stuck, nor breath nor motion ;

As idle as a painted ship
Upon a painted ocean.

"Water, water everywhere,
And all the boards did shrink;
Water, water everywhere,
Nor any drop to drink.

"About, about, in reel and rout
The death-fires danced at night;
The water, like a witch's oils,
Burnt green, and blue, and white.

"And every tongue, through utter drought,
Was withered at the root;
We could not speak, no more than if
We had been choked with soot.

"Ah! well-a-day! what evil looks
Had I from old and young!
Instead of the cross, the Albatross
About my neck was hung.

"There passed a weary time. Each throat
Was parched, and glazed each eye.
A weary time! a weary time!
How glazed each weary eye,
When looking westward, I beheld
A something in the sky.

"At first it seemed a little speck,
And then it seemed a mist;
It moved and moved, and took at last
A certain shape, I wist.

" A speck, a mist, a shape, I wist !
And still it neared and neared :
As if it dodged a water-sprite,
It plunged, and tacked, and veered.

"See ! see ! (I cried) she tacks no more !
Hither to work us weal ;
Without a breeze, without a tide,
She steadies with upright keel !

"The western wave was all a-flame,
The day was wellnigh done !
Almost upon the western wave
Rested the broad, bright Sun :
When that strange shape drove suddenly
Betwixt us and the Sun.

"And straight the Sun was flecked with bars,
(Heaven's Mother send us grace !)
As if through a dungeon grate he peered
With broad and burning face.

" Alas ! (thought I, and my heart beat loud)
How fast she nears and nears !
Are those her sails that glance in the Sun,
Like restless gossameres ?

" Are those her ribs through which the Sun
Did peer, as through a grate ?
And is that Woman all her crew ?
Is that a Death ? and are there two ?
Is Death that Woman's mate ?

"The naked hull alongside came,
And the twain were casting dice ;

'The game is done ! I 've won, I 've won !'
Quoth she, and whistles thrice.

"The Sun's rim dips ; the stars rush out :
At one stride comes the dark ;
With far-heard whisper o'er the sea,
Off shot the spectre-bark.

"The stars were dim and thick the night,
The steersman's face by his lamp gleamed white ;
From the sails the dew did drip —
Till clomb above the eastern bar
The horned Moon, with one bright star
Within the nether tip.

"Four times fifty living men,
(And I heard nor sigh nor groan,)
With heavy thump, a lifeless lump,
They dropped down one by one.

"The souls did from their bodies fly, —
They fled to bliss or woe !
And every soul, it passed me by,
Like the whizz of my cross-bow !

"The many men, so beautiful !
And they all dead did lie :
And a thousand thousand slimy things
Lived on ; and so did I.

"I looked upon the rotting sea,
And drew my eyes away ;
I looked upon the rotting deck,
And there the dead men lay.

" I looked to heaven, and tried to pray;
But or ever a prayer had gusht,
A wicked whisper came, and made
My heart as dry as dust.

" The moving Moon went up the sky,
And nowhere did abide :
Softly she was going up,
And a star or two beside.

" Beyond the shadow of the ship,
I watched the water-snakes :
They moved in tracks of shining white,
And when they reared, the elfish light
Fell off in hoary flakes.

" Within the shadow of the ship
I watched their rich attire :
Blue, glossy green, and velvet black,
They coiled and swam ; and every track
Was a flash of golden fire.

" O happy living things ! no tongue
Their beauty might declare :
A spring of love gushed from my heart,
And I blessed them unaware :
Sure my kind Saint took pity on me,
And I blessed them unaware.

" The selfsame moment I could pray ;
And from my neck so free
The Albatross fell off, and sank
Like lead into the sea.

5

"And soon I heard a roaring wind :
It did not come anear ;
But with its sound it shook the sails,
That were so thin and sere.

"The loud wind never reached the ship,
Yet now the ship moved on !
Beneath the lightning and the moon .
The dead men gave a groan.

"They groaned, they stirred, they all uprose,
Nor spake, nor moved their eyes ;
It had been strange, even in a dream,
To have seen those dead men rise.

"The helmsman steered, the ship moved on,
Yet never a breeze up blew ;
The mariners all 'gan work the ropes,
Where they were wont to do ;
They raised their limbs like lifeless tools —
We were a ghastly crew."

"I fear thee, ancient Mariner !"
"Be calm, thou Wedding-Guest !
'T was not those souls that fled in pain,
Which to their corses came again,
But a troop of spirits blest.

"Swiftly, swiftly flew the ship,
Yet she sailed softly too ;
Sweetly, sweetly blew the breeze —
On me alone it blew.

"Oh ! dream of joy ! is this indeed
The light-house top I see ?

45219

Is this the hill? is this the kirk?
Is this mine own countree?

" Since then, at an uncertain hour,
My agony returns :
And till my ghastly tale is told,
This heart within me burns.

" I pass, like night, from land to land ;
I have strange power of speech ;
That moment that his face I see,
I know the man that must hear me :
To him my tale I teach.

" What loud uproar bursts from that door !
The wedding-guests are there :
But in the garden-bower the bride
And bride-maids singing are :
And hark the little vesper bell,
Which biddeth me to prayer !

" O sweeter than the marriage-feast,
'T is sweeter far to me,
To walk together to the kirk
With a goodly company !

" To walk together to the kirk,
And all together pray,
While each to his great Father bends,
Old men, and babes, and loving friends,
And youths and maidens gay !

" Farewell, farewell ! but this I tell
To thee, thou Wedding-Guest !

He prayeth well, who loveth well
Both man and bird and beast.

" He prayeth best, who loveth best
All things both great and small ;
For the dear God who loveth us,
He made and loveth all."

S. T. Coleridge

XXXIX

SONG OF ARIEL

COME unto these yellow sands,
    And then take hands, —
Curtsied when you have and kiss'd ;
(The wild waves whist) —
Foot it featly here and there ;
And, sweet sprites, the burden bear.
    Hark, hark !
  Bough wough,
    The watch dogs bark,
  Bough wough,
Hark, hark ! I hear
The strain of strutting chanticleer,
Cry, cock-a-doodle-doo.

W. Shakespeare

XL

HOW'S MY BOY?

HO, sailor of the sea !
  How's my boy — my boy ?
'What's your boy's name, good wife,
And in what good ship sail'd he ?'

My boy John —
He that went to sea —
What care I for the ship, sailor ?
My boy's my boy to me.

You come back from sea
And not know my John ?
I might as well have asked some landsman
Yonder down in the town.
There's not an ass in all the parish
But he knows my John.

How's my boy — my boy ?
And unless you let me know
I'll swear you are no sailor,
Blue jacket or no,
Brass button or no, sailor,
Anchor and crown or no !
Sure his ship was the *Jolly Briton* —
'Speak low, woman, speak low !'

And why should I speak low, sailor ?
About my own boy John ?
If I was loud as I am proud
I'd sing him over the town !

Why should I speak low, sailor ?
' That good ship went down.'

How 's my boy — my boy ?
What care I for the ship, sailor,
I never was aboard her.
Be she afloat, or be she aground,
Sinking or swimming, I 'll be bound,
Her owners can afford her !
I say, how 's my John ?
' Every man on board went down,
Every man aboard her.'

How 's my boy — my boy ?
What care I for the men, sailor ?
I 'm not their mother —
How 's my boy — my boy ?
Tell me of him and no other !
How 's my boy — my boy ?

S. Dobell

XLI

THE SPANISH ARMADA

ATTEND all ye who list to hear our noble Eng-
land's praise,
I tell of the thrice famous deeds she wrought in ancient
days,
When the great fleet invincible against her bore in
vain
The richest stores of Mexico, the stoutest hearts of
Spain.

It was about the lovely close of a warm summer's
    day,
There came a gallant merchant-ship full sail to Plymouth
    Bay ;
Her crew hath seen Castile's black fleet beyond
    Aurigny's isle,
At earliest twilight, on the waves lie heaving many a
    mile ;
At sunset she escaped their van, by God's especial
    grace ;
And the tall Pinta, till the noon, had held her close
    in chase.
Forthwith a guard at every gun was placed along the
    wall ;
The beacon blazed upon the roof of Edgcumbe's lofty
    hall ;
Many a light fishing-bark put out to pry along the
    coast ;
And with loose rein and bloody spur rode inland many
    a post.
With his white hair unbonneted the stout old sheriff
    comes ;
Behind him march the halberdiers, before him sound
    the drums ;
His yeomen, round the market-cross, make clear an
    ample space,
For there behoves him to set up the standard of her
    Grace.
And haughtily the trumpets peal, and gayly dance the
    bells,
As slow upon the labouring wind the royal blazon
    swells.
Look how the lion of the sea lifts up his ancient
    crown,

And underneath his deadly paw treads the gay lilies
    down.
So stalked he when he turned to flight, on that famed
    Picard field,
Bohemia's plume, and Genoa's bow, and Cæsar's eagle
    shield :
So glared he when at Agincourt in wrath he turned
    to bay,
And crushed and torn beneath his paws the princely
    hunters lay.
Ho ! strike the flag-staff deep, Sir Knight ; ho ! scatter
    flowers, fair maids :
Ho ! gunners fire a loud salute ; ho ! gallants, draw
    your blades ;
Thou sun, shine on her joyously — ye breezes waft her
    wide ;
Our glorious SEMPER EADEM — the banner of
    our pride.
The freshening breeze of eve unfurled that banner's
    massive fold,
The parting gleam of sunshine kissed that haughty
    scroll of gold ;
Night sank upon the dusky beach, and on the purple
    sea, —
Such night in England ne'er had been, nor ne'er again
    shall be.
From Eddystone to Berwick bounds, from Lynn to
    Milford Bay,
That time of slumber was as bright and busy as the
    day ;
For swift to east and swift to west the warning radi-
    ance spread ;
High on St. Michael's Mount it shone — it shone on
    Beachy Head.

Far on the deep the Spaniard saw, along each south-
    ern shire,
Cape beyond cape, in endless range, those twinkling
    points of fire ;
The fisher left his skiff to rock on Tamar's glittering
    waves,
The rugged miners poured to war from Mendip's sun-
    less caves.
O'er Longleat's towers, o'er Cranbourne's oaks, the
    fiery herald flew ;
He roused the shepherds of Stonehenge, the rangers
    of Beaulieu.
Right sharp and quick the bells all night rang out from
    Bristol town,
And ere the day three hundred horse had met on
    Clifton down ;
The sentinel on Whitehall gate looked forth into the
    night,
And saw, o'erhanging Richmond Hill, the streak of
    blood-red light.
Then bugle's note and cannon's roar the death-like
    silence broke,
And with one start, and with one cry, the royal city
    woke.
At once on all her stately gates arose the answering
    fires ;
At once the loud alarum clashed from all her reeling
    spires ;
From all the batteries of the Tower pealed loud the
    voice of fear ;
And all the thousand masts of Thames sent back a
    louder cheer :
And from the farthest wards was heard the rush of
    hurrying feet,

And the broad streams of flags and pikes dashed down
    each roaring street :

And broader still became the blaze, and louder still the
    din,

As fast from every village round the horse came spur-
    ring in :

And eastward straight, from wild Blackheath, the war-
    like errand went,

And raised in many an ancient hall the gallant squires
    of Kent.

Southward, from Surrey's pleasant hills flew those
    bright couriers forth ;

High on bleak Hampstead's swarthy moor they started
    for the North ;

And on, and on, without a pause, untired they bounded
    still,

All night from tower to tower they sprang — they
    sprang from hill to hill,

Till the proud Peak unfurled the flag o'er Darwin's
    rocky dales —

Till like volcanoes flared to Heaven the stormy hills
    of Wales —

Till twelve fair counties saw the blaze on Malvern's
    lonely height —

Till streamed in crimson on the wind the Wrekin's
    crest of light —

Till broad and fierce the star came forth on Ely's
    stately fane,

And tower and hamlet rose in arms o'er all the bound-
    less plain ;

Till Belvoir's lordly terraces the sign to Lincoln
    sent,

And Lincoln sped the message on o'er the wide vale
    of Trent ;

Till Skiddaw saw the fire that burned on Gaunt's em-
        battled pile,
And the red glare of Skiddaw roused the burghers of
        Carlisle.

> *Lord Macaulay*

XLII

THE TAR FOR ALL WEATHERS

I SAIL'D from the Downs in the *Nancy*,
    My jib how she smack'd through the breeze !
She's a vessel as tight to my fancy
    As ever sail'd on the salt seas,
So adieu to the white cliffs of Britain,
    Our girls and our dear native shore !
For if some hard rock we should split on,
    We shall never see them any more.
But sailors were born for all weathers,
    Great guns let it blow, high or low,
Our duty keeps us to our tethers,
    And where the gale drives we must go.

When we entered the Straits of Gibraltar
    I verily thought she'd have sunk,
For the wind began so for to alter,
    She yaw'd just as tho' she was drunk.
The squall tore the mainsail to shivers,
    Helm a-weather, the hoarse boatswain cries ;
Brace the foresail athwart, see she quivers,
    As through the rough tempest she flies.
But sailors were born for all weathers,
    Great guns let it blow, high or low,

Our duty keeps us to our tethers,
  And where the gale drives we must go.

The storm came on thicker and faster,
  As black just as pitch was the sky,
When truly a doleful disaster
  Befell three poor sailors and I.
Ben Buntline, Sam Shroud, and Dick Handsail,
  By a blast that came furious and hard,
Just while we were furling the mainsail,
  Were every soul swept from the yard.
But sailors were born for all weathers,
  Great guns let it blow, high or low,
Our duty keeps us to our tethers,
  And where the gale drives we must go.

Poor Ben, Sam, and Dick cried peccavi,
  As for I, at the risk of my neck,
While they sank down in peace to old Davy,
  Caught a rope, and so landed on deck.
Well, what would you have? We were stranded,
  And out of a fine jolly crew
Of three hundred that sail'd, never landed
  But I, and I think, twenty-two.
But sailors were born for all weathers,
  Great guns let it blow, high or low,
Our duty keeps us to our tethers,
  And where the gale drives we must go.
                                    C. Dibdin

XLIII

THE FISHERMAN

A PERILOUS life, and sad as life may be,
  Hath the lone fisher, on the lonely sea,
O'er the wild waters labouring far from home,
For some bleak pittance e'er compelled to roam :
Few hearts to cheer him through his dangerous life,
And none to aid him in the stormy strife :
Companion of the sea and silent air,
The lonely fisher thus must ever fare :
Without the comfort, hope, — with scarce a friend,
He looks through life and only sees its end !

B. Cornwall

XLIV

THE SAILOR

THOU that hast a daughter
  For one to woo and wed,
Give her to a husband
  With snow upon his head :
Oh, give her to an old man,
  Though little joy it be,
Before the best young sailor
  That sails upon the sea !

How luckless is the sailor
  When sick and like to die,
He sees no tender mother,
  No sweetheart standing by.

Only the captain speaks to him, —
   Stand up, stand up, young man,
And steer the ship to haven,
   As none beside thee can.

Thou sayst to me, ' Stand, stand up';
   I say to thee, take hold,
Lift me a little from the deck,
   My hands and feet are cold.
And let my head, I pray thee,
   With handkerchiefs be bound :
There, take my love's gold handkerchief,
   And tie it tightly round.

Now bring the chart, the doleful chart ;
   See where these mountains meet —
The clouds are thick around their head,
   The mists around their feet :
Cast anchor here ; 't is deep and safe
   Within the rocky cleft ;
The little anchor on the right,
   The great one on the left.

And now to thee, O captain,
   Most earnestly I pray,
That they may never bury me
   In church or cloister gray ;
But on the windy sea-beach,
   At the ending of the land,
All on the surfy sea-beach,
   Deep down into the sand.

For there will come the sailors,
   Their voices I shall hear,

And at casting of the anchor
  The yo-ho loud and clear ;
And at hauling of the anchor
  The yo-ho and the cheer, —
Farewell, my love, for to thy bay
  I never more may steer.
                              W. Allingham

XLV

THE WRECK OF THE HESPERUS

IT was the schooner *Hesperus*,
  That sail'd the wintry sea ;
And the skipper had taken his little daughter,
  To bear him company.

Blue were her eyes as the fairy flax,
  Her cheeks like the dawn of day,
And her bosom white as the hawthorn buds,
  That ope in the month of May.

The skipper he stood beside the helm,
  His pipe was in his mouth,
And he watch'd how the veering flaw did blow
  The smoke now west, now south.

Then up and spake an old sailor,
  Had sail'd the Spanish Main,
'I pray thee put into yonder port,
  For I fear the hurricane.

'Last night the moon had a golden ring,
  And to-night no moon we see !'

The skipper he blew a whiff from his pipe,
　And a scornful laugh laughed he.

Colder and louder blew the wind,
　A gale from the north-east ;
The snow fell hissing in the brine, ·
　And the billows frothed like yeast.

Down came the storm and smote amain
　The vessel in its strength ;
She shuddered and paused like a frighted steed,
　Then leaped her cable's length.

' Come hither ! come hither ! my little daughter,
　And do not tremble so ;
For I can weather the roughest gale,
　That ever wind did blow.'

He wrapped her warm in his seaman's coat,
　Against the stinging blast ;
He cut a rope from a broken spar,
　And bound her to the mast.

' O father ! I hear the church bells ring,
　O say, what may it be ?'
' 'T is a fog-bell on a rock-bound coast !'
　And he steered for the open sea.

' O father ! I hear the sound of guns,
　O say, what may it be ?'
' Some ship in distress that cannot live
　In such an angry sea !'

' O father ! I see a gleaming light,
　O say, what may it be ?'

But the father answered never a word, —
　　A frozen corpse was he.

Lashed to the helm, all stiff and stark,
　　With his face turn'd to the skies,
The lantern gleam'd through the gleaming snow
　　On his fixed and glassy eyes.

Then the maiden clasped her hands and prayed
　　That savèd she might be ;
And she thought of Christ who stilled the waves
　　On the Lake of Galilee.

And fast through the midnight dark and drear,
　　Through the whistling sleet and snow,
Like a sheeted ghost the vessel swept
　　Tow'rds the reef of Norman's Woe.

And ever the fitful gusts between
　　A sound came from the land ;
It was the sound of the trampling surf
　　On the rocks and the hard sea-sand.

The breakers were right beneath her bows,
　　She drifted a dreary wreck,
And a whooping billow swept the crew
　　Like icicles from her deck.

She struck where the white and fleecy waves
　　Look'd soft as carded wool,
But the cruel rocks they gored her sides
　　Like the horns of an angry bull.

Her rattling shrouds all sheathed in ice,
　　With the masts went by the board ;
　　6

Like a vessel of glass she stove and sank,
  Ho ! ho ! the breakers roared.

At day-break on the bleak sea-beach,
  A fisherman stood aghast,
To see the form of a maiden fair
  Lashed close to a drifting mast.

The salt sea was frozen on her breast,
  The salt tears in her eyes ;
And he saw her hair, like the brown sea-weed,
  On the billows fall and rise.

Such was the wreck of the *Hesperus*,
  In the midnight and the snow ;
Heaven save us all from a death like this,
  On the reef of Norman's Woe !

  H. W. Longfellow

XLVI

A CANADIAN BOAT SONG

FAINTLY as tolls the evening chime,
  Our voices keep tune and our oars keep time.
Soon as the woods on the shore look dim,
We 'll sing at St. Anne's our parting hymn.
Row, brothers, row, the stream runs fast,
The Rapids are near and the daylight 's past.

  Why should we yet our sail unfurl ?
There is not a breath the blue wave to curl ;
But when the wind blows off the shore,
Oh ! sweetly we 'll rest our weary oar.

Blow, breezes, blow, the stream runs fast,
The Rapids are near and the daylight's past.

Utawa's tide ! this trembling moon
Shall see us float over thy surges soon.
Saint of this green isle ! hear our prayers,
Oh, grant us cool heavens, and favouring airs.
Blow, breezes, blow, the stream runs fast,
The Rapids are near and the daylight's past.

T. Moore

XLVII

ROSABELLE

O LISTEN, listen, ladies gay !
   No haughty feat of arms I tell ;
Soft is the note, and sad the lay,
   That mourns the lovely Rosabelle.

' Moor, moor the barge, ye gallant crew,
   And gentle lady, deign to stay !
Rest thee in Castle Ravensheuch,
   Nor tempt the stormy firth to-day.

' The blackening wave is edged with white ;
   To inch and rock the sea-mews fly ;
The fishers have heard the Water-Sprite,
   Whose screams forebode that wreck is nigh.

' Last night the gifted seer did view
   A wet shroud swathed round lady gay ;
Then stay thee, Fair, in Ravensheuch ;
   Why cross the gloomy firth to-day ? '

' 'T is not because Lord Lindesay's heir
   To-night at Roslin leads the ball,
But that my lady-mother there
   Sits lonely in her castle hall.

' 'T is not because the ring they ride,
   And Lindesay at the ring rides well,
But that my sire the wine will chide
   If 't is not fill'd by Rosabelle.'

— O'er Roslin all that dreary night
   A wondrous blaze was seen to gleam ;
'T was broader than the watch-fire's light,
   And redder than the bright moonbeam.

It glared on Roslin's castled rock,
   It ruddied all the copse-wood glen ;
'T was seen from Dryden's groves of oak,
   And seen from cavern'd Hawthornden.

Seem'd all on fire that chapel proud
   Where Roslin's chiefs uncoffin'd lie,
Each Baron, for a sable shroud,
   Sheath'd in his iron panoply.

Seem'd all on fire within, around,
   Deep sacristy and altar's pale ;
Shone every pillar foliage-bound,
   And glimmer'd all the dead men's mail.

Blazed battlement and pinnet high,
   Blazed every rose-carved buttress fair —
So still they blaze, when fate is nigh
   The lordly line of high St. Clair.

There are twenty of Roslin's barons bold
    Lie buried within that proud chapelle ;
Each one the holy vault doth hold,
    But the sea holds lovely Rosabelle !

And each St. Clair was buried there
    With candle, with book, and with knell ;
But the sea-caves rung, and the wild winds sung,
    The dirge of lovely Rosabelle.

Sir W. Scott

XLVIII

THE BALLAD OF THE BOAT

THE stream was smooth as glass, we said, 'Arise
    and let 's away' :
The Siren sang beside the boat that in the rushes lay ;
And spread the sail, and strong the oar, we gayly took
    our way.
When shall the sandy bar be cross'd ? when shall we
    find the bay ?

The broadening flood swells slowly out o'er cattle-dot-
    ted plains,
The stream is strong and turbulent, and dark with
    heavy rains ;
The labourer looks up to see our shallop speed away.
When shall the sandy bar be cross'd ? when shall we
    find the bay ?

Now are the clouds like fiery shrouds ; the sun, superb-
    ly large,
Slow as an oak to woodman's stroke sinks flaming at
    their marge.

The waves are bright with mirror'd light as jacinths on
our way.
When shall the sandy bar be cross'd? when shall we
find the bay?

The moon is high up in the sky, and now no more we
see
The spreading river's either bank, and surging dis-
tantly
There booms a sullen thunder as of breakers far
away.
Now shall the sandy bar be cross'd, now shall we find
the bay!

The sea-gull shrieks high overhead, and dimly to our
sight
The moonlit crests of foaming waves gleam towering
through the night.
We'll steal upon the mermaid soon, and start her from
her lay,
When once the sandy bar is cross'd, and we are in the
bay.

What rises white and awful as a shroud-enfolded
ghost?
What roar of rampant tumult bursts in clangour on
the coast?
Pull back! pull back! The raging flood sweeps every
oar away.
O stream, is this thy bar of sand? O boat, is this the
bay?

R. Garnett

XLIX

VERSES

Supposed to be written by Alexander Selkirk, during his solitary abode in the Island of Juan Fernandez

I AM monarch of all I survey,
　My right there is none to dispute ;
From the centre all round to the sea,
　'I am lord of the fowl and the brute.
O Solitude ! where are the charms
　That sages have seen in thy face ?
Better dwell in the midst of alarms
　Than reign in this horrible place.

I am out of humanity's reach,
　I must finish my journey alone,
Never hear the sweet music of speech,
　I start at the sound of my own.
The beasts that roam over the plain
　My form with indifference see ;
They are so unacquainted with man,
　Their tameness is shocking to me.

Society, friendship, and love,
　Divinely bestowed upon man,
O, had I the wings of a dove,
　How soon would I taste you again !
My sorrows I then might assuage,
　In the ways of religion and truth,
Might learn from the wisdom of age,
　And be cheer'd by the sallies of youth.

Religion ! what treasure untold
　Lies hid in that heavenly word !

More precious than silver or gold,
　Or all that this earth can afford.
But the sound of the church-going bell
　These valleys and rocks never heard,
Never sigh'd at the sound of a knell,
　Or smiled when a sabbath appear'd.

Ye winds that have made me your sport,
　Convey to this desolate shore
Some cordial, endearing report
　Of a land I shall visit no more.
My friends, do they now and then send
　A wish or a thought after me?
O, tell me I yet have a friend,
　Though a friend I am never to see.

How fleet is a glance of the mind!
　Compar'd with the speed of its flight,
The tempest himself lags behind
　And the swift-winged arrows of light.
When I think of my own native land,
　In a moment I seem to be there;
But, alas! recollection at hand
　Soon hurries me back to despair.

But the sea-fowl is gone to her nest,
　The beast is laid down in his lair;
Even here is a season of rest,
　And I to my cabin repair.
There's mercy in every place,
　And mercy, encouraging thought,
Gives even affliction a grace,
　And reconciles man to his lot.

W. Cowper

L

HOME THOUGHTS FROM ABROAD

OH, to be in England
　　Now that April 's there,
And whoever wakes in England
Sees, some morning, unaware,
That the lowest boughs and the brushwood sheaf
Round the elm-tree bole are in tiny leaf,
While the chaffinch sings on the orchard bough
In England — now !

And after April, when May follows,
And the white-throat builds, and all the swallows —
Hark ! where my blossomed pear-tree in the hedge
Leans to the field and scatters on the clover
Blossoms and dew-drops — at the bent spray's edge —
That 's the wise thrush ; he sings each song twice over,
Lest you should think he never could re-capture
The first fine careless rapture !
And though the fields look rough with hoary dew,
All will be gay when noontide wakes anew
The buttercups, the little children's dower,
— Far brighter than this gaudy melon-flower !
　　　　　　　　　　　　R. Browning

LI

THE DREAM OF EUGENE ARAM

'TWAS in the prime of summer time,
    An evening calm and cool,
And four-and-twenty happy boys
    Came bounding out of school :
There were some that ran, and some that leapt,
    Like troutlets in a pool.

Away they sped with gamesome minds,
    And souls untouch'd by sin ;
To a level mead they came, and there
    They drave the wickets in ;
Pleasantly shone the setting sun
    Over the town of Lynn.

Like sportive deer they coursed about,
    And shouted as they ran —
Turning to mirth all things of earth,
    As only boyhood can :
But the usher sat remote from all,
    A melancholy man !

His hat was off, his vest apart,
    To catch heaven's blessed breeze ;
For a burning thought was in his brow,
    And his bosom ill at ease ;
So he lean'd his head on his hands, and read
    The book between his knees !

Leaf after leaf he turn'd it o'er,
    Nor ever glanced aside ;

For the peace of his soul he read that book
  In the golden eventide :
Much study had made him very lean,
  And pale, and leaden-eyed.

At last he shut the ponderous tome ;
  With a fast and fervent grasp
He strain'd the dusky covers close,
  And fix'd the brazen hasp :
'O Heav'n, could I so close my mind,
  And clasp it with a clasp !'

Then leaping on his feet upright,
  Some moody turns he took ;
Now up the mead, then down the mead,
  And past a shady nook :
And lo ! he saw a little boy
  That pored upon a book !

'My gentle lad, what is 't you read —
  Romance or fairy fable ?
Or is it some historic page
  Of kings and crowns unstable ?'
The young boy gave an upward glance —
  'It is the death of Abel.'

The usher took six hasty strides,
  As smit with sudden pain ;
Six hasty strides beyond the place,
  Then slowly back again :
And down he sat beside the lad,
  And talked with him of Cain ;

And long since then, of bloody men,
  Whose deeds tradition saves ;

Of lonely folk cut off unseen,
   And hid in sudden graves ;
Of horrid stabs in groves forlorn,
   And murders done in caves ;

And how the sprites of injured men
   Shriek upward from the sod —
Ay, how the ghostly hand will point
   To show the burial clod ;
And unknown facts of guilty acts
   Are seen in dreams from God !

He told how murderers walk'd the earth
   Beneath the curse of Cain —
With crimson clouds before their eyes,
   And flames about their brain :
For blood has left upon their souls
   Its everlasting stain !

' And well,' quoth he, ' I know, for truth,
   Their pangs must be extreme —
Woe, woe, unutterable woe —
   Who spill life's sacred stream!
For why ?   Methought last night I wrought
   A murder in a dream !

' One that had never done me wrong —
   A feeble man, and old ;
I led him to a lonely field,
   The moon shone clear and cold :
Now here, said I, this man shall die,
   And I will have his gold !

Two sudden blows with a ragged stick,
   And one with a heavy stone,

One hurried gash with a hasty knife,
  And then the deed was done :
There was nothing lying at my feet,
  But lifeless flesh and bone !

' Nothing but lifeless flesh and bone,
  That could not do me ill ;
And yet I fear'd him all the more,
  For lying there so still :
There was a manhood in his look
  That murder could not kill !

' And lo ! the universal air
  Seem'd lit with ghastly flame —
Ten thousand, thousand dreadful eyes
  Were looking down in blame :
I took the dead man by the hand,
  And call'd upon his name !

' Oh me, it made me quake to see
  Such sense within the slain !
But when I touch'd the lifeless clay,
  The blood gush'd out amain !
For every clot, a burning spot
  Was scorching in my brain !

' My head was like an ardent coal,
  My heart as solid ice ;
My wretched, wretched soul, I knew,
  Was at the devil's price :
A dozen times I groan'd ; the dead
  Had never groan'd but twice !

' And now from forth the frowning sky,
  From the heaven's topmost height,

I heard a voice — the awful voice
  Of the blood-avenging sprite :
"Thou guilty man, take up thy dead,
  And hide it from my sight ! "

' I took the dreary body up
  And cast it in a stream —
A sluggish water, black as ink,
  The depth was so extreme.
My gentle boy, remember this
  Is nothing but a dream !

' Down went the corse with a hollow plunge,
  And vanish'd in the pool ;
Anon I cleansed my bloody hands,
  And wash'd my forehead cool,
And sat among the urchins young
  That evening in the school !

' O heaven, to think of their white souls,
  And mine so black and grim !
I could not share in childish prayer,
  Nor join in evening hymn :
Like a devil of the pit I seem'd,
  'Mid holy cherubim !

' And peace went with them, one and all,
  And each calm pillow spread ;
But Guilt was my grim chamberlain
  That lighted me to bed,
And drew my midnight curtains round,
  With fingers bloody red !

' All night I lay in agony,
  In anguish dark and deep ;

My fever'd eyes I dared not close,
　But star'd aghast at Sleep ;
For sin had render'd unto her
　The keys of hell to keep !

'All night I lay in agony,
　From weary chime to chime,
With one besetting horrid hint,
　That rack'd me all the time —
A mighty yearning, like the first
　Fierce impulse unto crime !

'One stern tyrannic thought that made
　All other thoughts its slave ;
Stronger and stronger every pulse
　Did that temptation crave —
Still urging me to go and see
　The dead man in his grave !

'Heavily I rose up — as soon
　As light was in the sky —
And sought the black accursed pool
　With a wild misgiving eye ;
And I saw the dead, in the river bed,
　For the faithless stream was dry !

'Merrily rose the lark, and shook
　The dew-drop from its wing ;
But I never mark'd its morning flight,
　I never heard it sing :
For I was stooping once again
　Under the horrid thing.

'With breathless speed, like a soul in chase,
　I took him up and ran —

There was no time to dig a grave
  Before the day began :
In a lonesome wood, with heaps of leaves,
  I hid the murder'd man !

' And all that day I read in school,
  But my thought was otherwhere !
As soon as the midday task was done,
  In secret I was there :
And a mighty wind had swept the leaves,
  And still the corse was bare !

' Then down I cast me on my face,
  And first began to weep ;
For I knew my secret then was one
  That earth refused to keep ;
Or land, or sea, though he should be
  Ten thousand fathoms deep !

' So wills the fierce avenging sprite,
  Till blood for blood atones !
Ay, though he 's buried in a cave,
  And trodden down with stones,
And years have rotted off his flesh —
  The world shall see his bones !

' Oh me ! that horrid, horrid dream
  Besets me now awake !
Again, again, with a dizzy brain,
  The human life I take ;
And my red right hand grows raging hot,
  Like Cranmer's at the stake.

' And still no peace for the restless clay
  Will wave or mould allow ;

The horrid thing pursues my soul —
  It stands before me now ! '
The fearful boy looked up and saw
  Huge drops upon his brow !

That very night, while gentle sleep
  The urchin eyelids kiss'd,
Two stern-faced men set out from Lynn,
  Through the cold and heavy mist ;
And Eugene Aram walk'd between,
  With gyves upon his wrist.

                          T. Hood

LII

THE BELEAGUERED CITY

BESIDE the Moldau's rushing stream,
  With the wan moon overhead,
There stood, as in an awful dream,
  The army of the dead.

White as a sea-fog, landward bound,
  The spectral camp was seen,
And with a sorrowful deep sound,
  The river flow'd between.

No other voice nor sound was there,
  No drum, nor sentry's pace ;
The mist-like banners clasp'd the air,
  As clouds with clouds embrace.

But when the old cathedral bell
  Proclaim'd the morning prayer,

7

The wild pavilions rose and fell
　On the alarmed air.

Down the broad valley fast and far,
　The troubled army fled ;
Up rose the glorious morning star,
　The ghastly host was dead.
　　*　　*　　*　　*H. W. Longfellow*

LIII

JAFFAR

JAFFAR, the Barmecide, the good Vizier,
　The poor man's hope, the friend without a peer.
Jaffar was dead, slain by a doom unjust ;
And guilty Haroun, sullen with mistrust
Of what the good, and e'en the bad might say,
Ordain'd that no man living from that day
Should dare to speak his name on pain of death.
All Araby and Persia held their breath.

All but the brave Mondeer. — He, proud to show
How far for love a grateful soul could go,
And facing death for very scorn and grief,
(For his great heart wanted a great relief,)
Stood forth in Bagdad, daily in the square
Where once had stood a happy house, and there
Harangued the tremblers at the scymitar
On all they owed to the divine Jaffar.

' Bring me this man,' the caliph cried : the man
Was brought, was gazed upon. The mutes began

To bind his arms.   ' Welcome, brave cords,' cried he ;
' From bonds far worse Jaffar deliver'd me ;
From wants, from shames, from loveless household
    fears ;
Made a man's eyes friends with delicious tears ;
Restor'd me, loved me, put me on a par
With his great self.   How can I pay Jaffar ? '

Haroun, who felt that on a soul like this
The mightiest vengeance could but fall amiss,
Now deigned to smile, as one great lord of fate
Might smile upon another half as great.
He said, ' Let worth grow frenzied if it will ;
The caliph's judgment shall be master still.
Go, and since gifts so move thee, take this gem,
The richest in the Tartar's diadem,
And hold the giver as thou deemest fit.'
' Gifts ! ' cried the friend.   He took ; and holding it
High toward the heavens, as though to meet his star,
Exclaim'd, ' This, too, I owe to thee, Jaffar.'

Leigh Hunt

LIV

COLIN AND LUCY

THREE times, all in the dead of night,
    A bell was heard to ring ;
And shrieking at the window thrice,
    The raven flapp'd his wing.
Too well the love-lorn maiden knew
    The solemn boding sound ;
And thus, in dying words bespoke,
    The virgins weeping round :

'I hear a voice you cannot hear,
  Which says I must not stay ;
I see a hand you cannot see,
  Which beckons me away.
By a false heart and broken vows,
  In early youth I die :
Was I to blame, because his bride
  Was thrice as rich as I ?

'Ah, Colin, give not her thy vows,
  Vows due to me alone :
Nor thou, fond maid, receive his kiss,
  Nor think him all thy own.
To-morrow in the church to wed,
  Impatient, both prepare !
But know, fond maid, and know, false man,
  That Lucy will be there !

'Then bear my corse, my comrades, bear,
  This bridegroom blithe to meet,
He, in his wedding trim so gay,
  I, in my winding-sheet.'
She spoke, she died, her corse was borne
  The bridegroom blithe to meet,
He in his wedding trim so gay,
  She in her winding-sheet.

Then what were perjur'd Colin's thoughts ?
  How were these nuptials kept ?
The bridesmen flock'd round Lucy dead,
  And all the village wept.
Confusion, shame, remorse, despair,
  At once his bosom swell :
The damps of death bedew'd his brow,
  He shook, he groan'd, he fell.

                              T. Tickell

LV

THE REDBREAST CHASING THE BUTTERFLY

ART thou the bird whom man loves best,
The pious bird with the scarlet breast,
Our little English robin?
The bird that comes about our doors
When autumn winds are sobbing?
Art thou the Peter of Norway boors?
Their Thomas in Finland,
And Russia far inland?
The bird, that by some name or other
All men who know thee call their brother:
The darling of children and men?
Could father Adam open his eyes,
And see this sight beneath the skies,
He'd wish to close them again.
— If the butterfly knew but his friend,
Hither his flight he would bend;
And find his way to me,
Under the branches of the tree:
In and out, he darts about;
Can this be the bird to man so good,
That after their bewildering,
Cover'd with leaves the little children,
So painfully in the wood?
What ail'd thee, robin, that thou couldst pursue
A beautiful creature,
That is gentle by nature?
Beneath the summer sky,
From flower to flower let him fly;
'T is all that he wishes to do.

The cheerer, thou, of our in-door sadness,
He is the friend of our summer gladness :
What hinders, then, that ye should be
Playmates in the sunny weather,
And fly about in the air together?
His beautiful wings in crimson are drest,
A crimson as bright as thine own :
Wouldst thou be happy in thy nest,
O pious bird ! whom man loves best,
Love him, or leave him alone !

W. Wordsworth

LVI

THE CHILDREN IN THE WOOD

NOW ponder well, you parents dear,
    These words which I shall write ;
A doleful story you shall hear,
    In time brought forth to light.
A gentleman of good account
    In Norfolk dwelt of late,
Who did in honour far surmount
    Most men of his estate.

Sore sick he was, and like to die,
    No help his life could save ;
His wife by him as sick did lie,
    And both possess'd one grave.
No love between these two was lost,
    Each was to other kind ;
In love they lived, in love they died,
    And left two babes behind.

The one, a fine and pretty boy,
    Not passing three years old ;
The other, a girl more young than he,
    And framed in beauty's mould.
The father left his little son,
    As plainly doth appear,
When he to perfect age should come,
    Three hundred pounds a year.

And to his little daughter Jane,
    Five hundred pounds in gold,
To be paid down on her marriage-day,
    Which might not be controll'd :
But if the children chanced to die
    Ere they to age should come,
Their uncle should possess their wealth ;
    For so the will did run.

'Now, brother,' said the dying man,
    'Look to my children dear ;
Be good unto my boy and girl,
    No friends else have they here :
To God and you I recommend
    My children dear this day ;
But little while be sure we have
    Within this world to stay.

'You must be father and mother both,
    And uncle all in one ;
God knows what will become of them,
    When I am dead and gone.'
With that bespake their mother dear,
    'O brother kind,' quoth she,
'You are the man must bring our babes
    To wealth or misery.

'And if you keep them carefully,
    Then God will you reward ;
But if you otherwise should deal,
    God will your deeds regard.'
With lips as cold as any stone,
    They kiss'd their children small :
'God bless you both, my children dear';
    With that their tears did fall.

These speeches then their brother spake
    To this sick couple there :
'The keeping of your little ones,
    Sweet sister, do not fear.
God never prosper me nor mine,
    Nor aught else that I have,
If I do wrong your children dear
    When you are laid in grave.'

The parents being dead and gone,
    The children home he takes,
And brings them straight unto his house,
    Where much of them he makes.
He had not kept these pretty babes
    A twelvemonth and a day,
But, for their wealth, he did devise
    To make them both away.

He bargain'd with two ruffians strong
    Which were of furious mood,
That they should take these children young
    And slay them in a wood.
He told his wife an artful tale :
    He would the children send
To be brought up in fair London,
    With one that was his friend.

Away then went those pretty babes,
   Rejoicing at that tide,
Rejoicing with a merry mind,
   They should on cock-horse ride.
They prate and prattle pleasantly,
   As they rode on the way,
To those that should their butchers be,
   And work their lives' decay.

So that the pretty speech they had,
   Made murder's heart relent :
And they that undertook the deed
   Full sore did now repent.
Yet one of them, more hard of heart,
   Did vow to do his charge,
Because the wretch that hired him
   Had paid him very large.

The other won't agree thereto,
   So here they fall to strife ;
With one another they did fight
   About the children's life :
And he that was of mildest mood,
   Did slay the other there,
Within an unfrequented wood :
   The babes did quake for fear !

He took the children by the hand,
   Tears standing in their eye,
And bade them straightway follow him,
   And look they did not cry ;
And two long miles he led them on,
   While they for food complain :
'Stay here,' quoth he, 'I'll bring you bread,
   When I come back again.'

These pretty babes, with hand in hand,
   Went wandering up and down ;
But never more could see the man
   Approaching from the town :
Their pretty lips with blackberries
   Were all besmear'd and dyed,
And when they saw the darksome night,
   They sat them down and cried.

Thus wandered these poor innocents
   Till death did end their grief,
In one another's arms they died,
   As wanting due relief :
No burial this pretty pair
   Of any man receives,
Till Robin Redbreast piously
   Did cover them with leaves.

And now the heavy wrath of God
   Upon their uncle fell ;
Yea, fearful fiends did haunt his house,
   His conscience felt an hell :
His barns were fired, his goods consumed,
   His lands were barren made,
His cattle died within the field,
   And nothing with him stayed.

And in the voyage to Portugal
   Two of his sons did die ;
And to conclude, himself was brought
   To want and misery.
He pawn'd and mortgaged all his land
   Ere seven years came about,
And now at length this wicked act
   Did by this means come out :

The fellow that did take in hand
   These children for to kill,
Was for a robbery judged to die,
   Such was God's blessed will.
Who did confess the very truth,
   As here hath been display'd :
Their uncle having died in gaol,
   Where he for debt was laid.

You that executors be made,
   And overseers eke
Of children that be fatherless,
   And infants mild and meek ;
Take you example by this thing,
   And yield to each his right,
Lest God with such like misery
   Your wicked minds requite.
               Old Ballad

LVII

ROBIN REDBREAST

GOOD-BYE, good-bye to Summer !
   For Summer's nearly done ;
The garden smiling faintly,
   Cool breezes in the sun ;
Our thrushes now are silent,
   Our swallows flown away, —
But Robin 's here in coat of brown,
   And scarlet breast-knot gay.
Robin, Robin Redbreast,
   O Robin dear !

Robin sings so sweetly
　　In the falling of the year.

Bright yellow, red, and orange,
　　The leaves come down in hosts ;
The trees are Indian princes,
　　But soon they 'll turn to ghosts ;
The leathery pears and apples
　　Hang russet on the bough ;
It 's Autumn, Autumn, Autumn late,
　　'T will soon be Winter now.
Robin, Robin Redbreast,
　　O Robin dear !
And what will this poor Robin do ?
　　For pinching days are near.

The fireside for the cricket,
　　The wheat-stack for the mouse,
When trembling night-winds whistle
　　And moan all round the house.
The frosty ways like iron,
　　The branches plumed with snow, —
Alas ! in winter dead and dark,
　　Where can poor Robin go ?
Robin, Robin Redbreast,
　　O Robin dear !
And a crumb of bread for Robin,
　　His little heart to cheer.

W. Allingham

LVIII

THE OWL

IN the hollow tree in the gray old tower,
   The spectral owl doth dwell ;
Dull, hated, despised in the sunshine hour,
   But at dusk — he 's abroad and well :
Not a bird of the forest e'er mates with him ;
   All mock him outright by day ;
But at night, when the woods grow still and dim,
   The boldest will shrink away ;
     O, when the night falls, and roosts the fowl,
     Then, then is the reign of the horned owl !

And the owl hath a bride who is fond and bold,
   And loveth the wood's deep gloom ;
And with eyes like the shine of the moonshine cold
   She awaiteth her ghastly groom !
Not a feather she moves, not a carol she sings,
   As she waits in her tree so still ;
But when her heart heareth his flapping wings,
   She hoots out her welcome shrill !
     O, when the moon shines, and the dogs do howl,
     Then, then is the cry of the horned owl !

Mourn not for the owl nor his gloomy plight !
   The owl hath his share of good :
If a prisoner he be in the broad daylight,
   He is lord in the dark green wood !
Nor lonely the bird, nor his ghastly mate ;
   They are each unto each a pride —
Thrice fonder, perhaps, since a strange dark fate
   Hath rent them from all beside !

So when the night falls, and dogs do howl,
    Sing Ho ! for the reign of the horned owl !
We know not alway who are kings by day,
    But the king of the night is the bold brown owl.
                                        B. Cornwall

LIX

HART-LEAP WELL

PART I

THE Knight had ridden down from Wensley Moor,
    With the slow motion of a summer's cloud,
And now, as he approach'd a vassal's door,
'Bring forth another horse !' he cried aloud.

'Another horse !' that shout the vassal heard,
And saddled his best steed, a comely gray ;
Sir Walter mounted him ; he was the third
Which he had mounted on that glorious day.

Joy sparkled in the prancing courser's eyes ;
The horse and horseman are a happy pair ;
But though Sir Walter like a falcon flies,
There is a doleful silence in the air.

A rout this morning left Sir Walter's Hall,
And as they galloped made the echoes roar ;
But horse and man are vanished, one and all ;
Such race, I think, was never seen before.

Sir Walter, restless as a veering wind,
Calls to the few tired dogs that yet remain ;

Blanche, Swift, and Music, noblest of their kind,
Follow, and up the weary mountain strain.

The Knight hallooed, he cheered and chid them on
With suppliant gestures and upbraidings stern ;
But breath and eyesight fail ; and, one by one,
The dogs are stretched among the mountain fern.

Where is the throng, the tumult of the race?
The bugles that so joyfully were blown?
This chase, it looks not like an earthly chase :
Sir Walter and the Hart are left alone.

The poor Hart toils along the mountain-side ;
I will not stop to tell how far he fled,
Nor will I mention by what death he died ;
But now the Knight beholds him lying dead.

Dismounting, then, he leaned against a thorn ;
He had no follower, dog, nor man, nor boy :
He neither cracked his whip nor blew his horn,
But gazed upon the spoil with silent joy.

Close to the thorn on which Sir Walter leaned,
Stood his dumb partner in this glorious feat ;
Weak as a lamb the hour that it is yeaned,
And white with foam as if with cleaving sleet :

Upon his side the Hart was lying stretched ;
His nostril touched a spring beneath a hill,
And with the last deep groan his breath had fetched,
The waters of the spring were trembling still.

And now, too happy for repose or rest,
(Never had living man such joyful lot !)

Sir Walter walked all round, north, south, and west,
And gazed, and gazed upon that darling spot.

And climbing up the hill, (it was at least
Four roods of sheer ascent,) Sir Walter found
Three several hoof-marks, which the hunted beast
Had left imprinted in the grassy ground.

Sir Walter wiped his face and cried, ' Till now
Such sight was never seen by human eyes ;
Three leaps have borne him from this lofty brow,
Down to the very fountain where he lies.

' I 'll build a pleasure house upon this spot,
And a small arbour made for rural joy ;
'T will be the traveller's shed, the pilgrim's cot,
A place of love for damsels that are coy.

' A cunning artist will I have to frame
A basin for that fountain in the dell !
And they who do make mention of the same,
From this day forth shall call it Hart-Leap Well.

' And, gallant stag, to make thy praises known,
Another monument shall here be raised ;
Three several pillars, each a rough hewn stone,
And planted where thy hoofs the turf have grazed.

' And in the summer time, when days are long,
I will come hither with my paramour,
And with the dancers and the minstrels' song,
We will make merry in that pleasant bower.

' Till the foundations of the mountains fail,
My mansion with its arbour shall endure ;

The joy of them who till the fields of Swale,
And them who dwell among the woods of Ure ! '

Then home he went and left the Hart, stone-dead,
With breathless nostrils stretch'd above the spring.
Soon did the Knight perform what he had said ;
And far and wide the fame thereof did ring.

Ere thrice the moon into her port had steered,
A cup of stone received the living well ;
Three pillars of rude stone Sir Walter reared,
And built a house for pleasure in the dell.

And near the fountain flowers of stature tall
With trailing plants and trees were intertwined, —
Which soon composed a little sylvan hall,
A leafy shelter from the sun and wind.

And thither, when the summer days were long,
Sir Walter led his wandering paramour,
And with the dancers and the minstrels' song,
Made merriment within that pleasant bower.

The Knight, Sir Walter, died in course of time,
And his bones lie in his paternal vale.
But there is matter for a second rhyme,
And I to this would add another tale.

PART II

The moving accident is not my trade ;
To freeze the blood I have no ready arts ;
'T is my delight, alone in summer shade,
To pipe a simple song to thinking hearts.

8

As I from Hawes to Richmond did repair,
It chanced that I saw standing in a dell
Three aspens at three corners of a square ;
And one, not four yards distant, near a well.

What this imported I could ill divine ;
And pulling now the rein my horse to stop,
I saw three pillars standing in a line, —
The last stone-pillar on a dark hill-top.

The trees were gray, with neither arms nor head ;
Half wasted the square mound of tawny green,
So that you might just say, as then I said,
'Here in old time the hand of man hath been.'

I looked upon the hill both far and near,
More doleful place did never eye survey ;
It seemed as if the spring-time came not here,
And Nature here were willing to decay.

I stood in various thoughts and fancies lost,
When one, who was in shepherd's garb attired,
Came up the hollow : — him I did accost,
And what this place might be I then inquired.

The Shepherd stopped, and that same story told
Which in my former rhyme I have rehearsed ;
'A jolly place,' said he, 'in times of old !
But something ails it now ; the spot is curst.

'You see those lifeless stumps of aspen wood —
Some say that they are beeches, others elms —
These were the bower ; and here a mansion stood,
The finest palace of a hundred realms !

'The arbour does its own condition tell ;
You see the stones, the fountain, and the stream ;
But as to the great lodge ! you might as well
Hunt half the day for a forgotten dream.

'There 's neither dog nor heifer, horse nor sheep,
Will wet his lips within that cup of stone ;
And oftentimes when all are fast asleep,
This water doth send forth a dolorous groan.

'Some say that here a murder has been done,
And blood cries out for blood ; but for my part
I 've guessed, when I 've been sitting in the sun,
That it was all for that unhappy Hart.

' What thoughts must through the creature's brain have
        past !
Even from the topmost stone upon the steep
Are but three bounds — and look, Sir, at this last —
O master ! it has been a cruel leap.

'For thirteen hours he ran a desperate race ;
And in my simple mind we cannot tell
What cause the Hart might have to love this place,
And come and make his death-bed near the well.

'Here on the grass, perhaps, asleep he sank,
Lulled by the fountain in the summer tide ;
This water was perhaps the first he drank,
When he had wandered from his mother's side.

'In April here beneath the flowering thorn,
He heard the birds their morning carols sing ;
And he, perhaps, for aught we know, was born
Not half a furlong from that self-same spring.

'Now here is neither grass nor pleasant shade ;
The sun on drearier hollow never shone ;
So will it be, as I have often said,
Till trees, and stones, and fountain all are gone.'

'Gray-headed Shepherd, thou hast spoken well ;
Small difference lies between thy creed and mine :
This beast not unobserved by Nature fell ;
His death was mourned by sympathy Divine.

'The Being that is in the clouds and air,
That is in the green leaves among the groves,
Maintains a deep and reverential care
For the unoffending creatures whom he loves.

'The pleasure house is dust, behind, before,
This is no common waste, no common gloom ;
But Nature, in due course of time, once more
Shall here put on her beauty and her bloom.

'She leaves these objects to a slow decay.
That what we are, and have been, may be known ;
But at the coming of a milder day,
These monuments shall all be overgrown.

'One lesson, Shepherd, let us two divide,
Taught both by what she shows and what conceals,
Never to blend our pleasure or our pride
With sorrow of the meanest thing that feels.'

W. Wordsworth

LX

THE SUMMER SHOWER

BEFORE the stout harvesters falleth the grain,
As when the strong storm-wind is reaping the
plain,
And loiters the boy in the briery lane ;
But yonder aslant comes the silvery rain,
Like a long line of spears brightly burnish'd and tall.

Adown the white highway like cavalry fleet,
It dashes the dust with its numberless feet.
Like a murmurless school, in their leafy retreat,
The wild birds sit listening the drops round them
beat ;
And the boy crouches close to the blackberry wall.

The swallows alone take the storm on their wing,
And, taunting the tree-sheltered labourers, sing,
Like pebbles the rain breaks the face of the spring,
While a bubble darts up from each widening ring ;
And the boy in dismay hears the loud shower fall.

But soon are the harvesters tossing their sheaves ;
The robin darts out from his bower of leaves ;
The wren peereth forth from the moss-covered eaves ;
And the rain-spatter'd urchin now gladly perceives
That the beautiful bow bendeth over them all.

T. B. Read

LXI

THE MOUSE'S PETITION

OH, hear a pensive prisoner's prayer,
　For liberty that sighs ;
And never let thine heart be shut
　Against the wretch's cries !

For here forlorn and sad I sit,
　Within the wiry grate ;
And tremble at the approaching morn,
　Which brings impending fate.

If e'er thy breast with freedom glowed,
　And spurned a tyrant's chain,
Let not thy strong oppressive force
　A free-born mouse detain !

Oh, do not stain with guiltless blood
　Thy hospitable hearth !
Nor triumph that thy wiles betrayed
　A prize so little worth.

The scattered gleanings of a feast
　My frugal meals supply ;
But if thy unrelenting heart
　That slender boon deny,—

The cheerful light, the vital air,
　Are blessings widely given ;
Let Nature's commoners enjoy
　The common gifts of heaven.

Beware, lest, in the worm you crush,
   A brother's soul you find ;
And tremble lest thy luckless hand
   Dislodge a kindred mind.

Or if this transient gleam of day
   Be *all* the life we share,
Let pity plead within thy breast,
   That little *all* to spare.

So may thy hospitable board
   With health and peace be crowned ;
And every charm of heartfelt ease
   Beneath thy roof be found.

So when destruction works unseen,
   Which man, like mice, may share,
May some kind angel clear thy path,
   And break the hidden snare.
                 A. L. Barbauld

LXII

THE GRASSHOPPER

HAPPY insect ! what can be
   In happiness compared to thee ?
Fed with nourishment divine,
The dewy morning's gentle wine !
Nature waits upon thee still,
And thy verdant cup does fill ;
'T is fill'd wherever thou dost tread,
Nature's self 's thy Ganymede.

Thou dost drink, and dance, and sing,
Happier than the happiest king!
All the fields which thou dost see,
All the plants belong to thee,
All that summer hours produce,
Fertile made with early juice:
Man for thee does sow and plough;
Farmer he and landlord thou!
Thou dost innocently joy,
Nor does thy luxury destroy.
The shepherd gladly heareth thee,
More harmonious than he.
Thee, country minds with gladness hear,
Prophet of the ripened year:
Thee Phœbus loves and does inspire;
Phœbus is himself thy sire.
To thee of all things upon earth,
Life is no longer than thy mirth.
Happy insect! happy thou,
Dost neither age nor winter know:
But when thou 'st drunk, and danced, and sung
Thy fill, the flowery leaves among,
(Voluptuous and wise withal,
Epicurean animal,)
Sated with the summer feast
Thou retir'st to endless rest.

A. Cowley

LXIII

THE SHEPHERD'S HOME

M Y banks they are furnished with bees,
  Whose murmur invites one to sleep;
My grottoes are shaded with trees,
  And my hills are white over with sheep.
I seldom have met with a loss,
  Such health do my fountains bestow;
My fountains all bordered with moss,
  Where the harebells and violets blow.

Not a pine in the grove is there seen,
  But with tendrils of woodbine is bound;
Not a beech's more beautiful green,
  But a sweet-brier entwines it around.
Not my fields in the prime of the year,
  More charms than my cattle unfold;
Not a brook that is limpid and clear,
  But it glitters with fishes of gold.

I have found out a gift for my fair,
  I have found where the wood-pigeons breed,
But let me such plunder forbear,
  She will say 't was a barbarous deed;
For he ne'er could be true, she averred,
  Who would rob a poor bird of its young;
And I loved her the more when I heard
  Such tenderness fall from her tongue.
                              W. Shenstone

LXIV

THE LORD OF BURLEIGH

IN her ear he whispers gaily,
   'If my heart by signs can tell,
Maiden, I have watched thee daily,
   And I think thou lov'st me well.'
She replies, in accents fainter,
   'There is none I love like thee.'
He is but a landscape painter,
   And a village maiden she.
He to lips that fondly falter,
   Presses his without reproof;
Leads her to the village altar,
   And they leave her father's roof.
'I can make no marriage present;
   Little can I give my wife:
Love will make our cottage pleasant,
   And I love thee more than life.'
They by parks and lodges going,
   See the lordly castles stand:
Summer woods about them blowing,
   Made a murmur in the land.
From deep thought himself he rouses,
   Says to her that loves him well,
'Let us see these handsome houses
   Where the wealthy nobles dwell.'
So she goes, by him attended,
   Hears him lovingly converse,
Sees whatever fair and splendid
   Lay betwixt his home and hers;

Parks with oak and chestnut shady,
  Parks and ordered gardens great,
Ancient homes of lord and lady,
  Built for pleasure and for state.
All he shows her makes him dearer :
  Evermore she seems to gaze
On that cottage growing nearer,
  Where they twain will spend their days.
O but she will love him truly !
  He shall have a cheerful home ;
She will order all things duly,
  When beneath his roof they come.
Thus her heart rejoices greatly,
  Till a gateway she discerns,
With armorial bearings stately,
  And beneath the gate she turns ;
Sees a mansion more majestic
  Than all those she saw before ;
Many a gallant gay domestic
  Bows before him at the door.
And they speak in gentle murmur,
  When they answer to his call,
While he treads with footsteps firmer,
  Leading on from hall to hall.
And while now she wonders blindly,
  Nor the meaning can divine,
Proudly turns he round and kindly,
  ' All of this is mine and thine.'
Here he lives in state and bounty,
  Lord of Burleigh, fair and free,
Not a lord in all the county
  Is so great a lord as he.
All at once the colour flushes
  Her sweet face from brow to chin :

As it were with shame she blushes,
 And her spirit changed within.
Then her countenance all over,
 Pale again as death did prove :
But he clasped her like a lover,
 And he cheered her soul with love.
So she strove against her weakness,
 Though at times her spirit sank :
Shaped her heart with woman's meekness,
 To all duties of her rank :
And a gentle consort made he,
 And her gentle mind was such,
That she grew a noble lady,
 And the people loved her much.
But a trouble weighed upon her,
 And perplexed her night and morn,
With the burden of an honour
 Unto which she was not born.
Faint she grew, and ever fainter,
 As she murmured, ' O that he
Were once more that landscape painter
 Which did win my heart from me !'
So she drooped and drooped before him,
 Fading slowly from his side :
Three fair children first she bore him,
 Then before her time she died.
Weeping, weeping late and early,
 Walking up and pacing down,
Deeply mourned the Lord of Burleigh,
 Burleigh House by Stamford town.
And he came to look upon her,
 And he looked at her, and said,
' Bring the dress, and put it on her,
 That she wore when she was wed.'

Then her people, softly treading,
   Bore to earth her body drest
In the dress that she was wed in,
   That her spirit might have rest.
                  A. Tennyson

LXV

THE MOUNTAIN AND THE SQUIRREL

THE mountain and the squirrel
   Had a quarrel,
And the former called the latter 'Little prig';
Bun replied,
'You are doubtless very big,
But all sorts of things and weather
Must be taken in together
To make up a year,
And a sphere.
And I think it no disgrace
To occupy my place.
If I'm not so large as you,
You are not so small as I,
And not half so spry :
I'll not deny you make
A very pretty squirrel track.
Talents differ ; all is well and wisely put ;
If I cannot carry forests on my back,
Neither can you crack a nut.'
                  R. W. Emerson

LXVI

EVENING

SHEPHERDS all, and maidens fair,
  Fold your flocks up, for the air
'Gins to thicken, and the sun
Already his great course has run.
See the dew-drops how they kiss
Every little flower that is,
Hanging on their velvet heads,
Like a rope of crystal beads.
See the heavy clouds low falling,
And bright Hesperus down calling
The dead night from underground,
At whose rising, mists unsound,
Damps and vapours fly apace,
Hovering o'er the wanton face
Of these pastures, where they come
Striking dead both bud and bloom.
Therefore from such danger lock
Every one of his loved flock ;
And let your dogs lie loose without,
Lest the wolf come, as a scout
From the mountain, and ere day
Bear a kid or lamb away ;
Or the crafty thievish fox
Break upon your simple flocks.
To secure yourselves from these,
Be not too secure in ease.
So shall you good shepherds prove,
And deserve your master's love.

Now, good night ! may sweetest slumbers
And soft silence fall in numbers
On your eyelids : so, farewell ;
Thus I end my evening knell.

J. Fletcher

LXVII

THE PARROT

A True Story

A PARROT, from the Spanish main,
   Full young and early caged came o'er,
With bright wings, to the bleak domain
   Of Mulla's shore.

To spicy groves where he had won
   His plumage of resplendent hue,
His native fruits, and skies, and sun,
   He bade adieu.

For these he changed the smoke of turf,
   A heathery land and misty sky,
And turned on rocks and raging surf
   His golden eye.

But petted in our climate cold,
   He lived and chattered many a day :
Until with age, from green and gold
   His wings grew gray.

At last when blind, and seeming dumb,
   He scolded, laugh'd, and spoke no more.

A Spanish stranger chanced to come
  To Mulla's shore ;

He hail'd the bird in Spanish speech,
  The bird in Spanish speech replied ;
Flapp'd round the cage with joyous screech,
  Dropt down, and died.

T. Campbell

LXVIII

SONG

I HAD a dove, and the sweet dove died ;
  And I have thought it died of grieving :
O, what could it grieve for ?   Its feet were tied
  With a silken thread of my own hand's weaving ;
Sweet little red feet ! why should you die —
Why would you leave me, sweet bird ! why ?
You lived alone in the forest tree,
Why, pretty thing ! would you not live with me ?
I kiss'd you oft and gave you white peas ;
Why not live sweetly, as in the green trees ?

J. Keats

LXIX

THE BLIND BOY

O SAY what is that thing called Light,
   Which I must ne'er enjoy ;
What are the blessings of the sight,
   O tell your poor blind boy !

You talk of wondrous things you see,
   You say the sun shines bright ;
I feel him warm, but how can he
   Or make it day or night ?

My day or night myself I make
   Whene'er I sleep or play ;
And could I ever keep awake
   With me 't were always day.

With heavy sighs I often hear
   You mourn my hapless woe ;
But sure with patience I can bear
   A loss I ne'er can know.

Then let not what I cannot have
   My cheer of mind destroy,
Whilst thus I sing, I am a king,
   Although a poor blind boy.

                C. Cibber

LXX

FALSE FRIENDS-LIKE

WHEN I was still a boy and mother's pride,
  A bigger boy spoke up to me so kind-like,
'If you do like, I 'll treat you with a ride
In this wheelbarrow.' So then I was blind-like
To what he had a-working in his mind-like,
And mounted for a passenger inside ;
And coming to a puddle, pretty wide,
He tipp'd me in a-grinning back behind-like.
So when a man may come to me so thick-like,
And shake my hand where once he pass'd me by,
And tell me he would do me this or that,
I can't help thinking of the big boy's trick-like,
And then, for all I can but wag my hat,
And thank him, I do feel a little shy.

W. Barnes

LXXI

GOODY BLAKE AND HARRY GILL

A True Story

OH ! what 's the matter ? what 's the matter ?
  What is 't that ails young Harry Gill,
That evermore his teeth they chatter,
Chatter, chatter, chatter still ?
Of waistcoats Harry has no lack,
Good duffil gray, and flannel fine ;
He has a blanket on his back,
And coats enough to smother nine.

In March, December, and in July,
'T is all the same with Harry Gill ;
The neighbours tell, and tell you truly,
His teeth they chatter, chatter still.
At night, at morning, and at noon,
'T is all the same with Harry Gill ;
Beneath the sun, beneath the moon,
His teeth they chatter, chatter still.

Young Harry was a lusty drover,
And who so stout of limb as he ?
His cheeks were red as ruddy clover ;
His voice was like the voice of three.
Old Goody Blake was old and poor ;
Ill fed she was and thinly clad ;
And any man who passed her door
Might see how poor a hut she had.

All day she spun in her poor dwelling :
And then her three hours' work at night,
Alas ! 't was hardly worth the telling,
It would not pay for candle-light.
Remote from sheltered village green,
On a hill's northern side she dwelt,
Where from sea-blasts the hawthorns lean,
And hoary dews are slow to melt.

By the same fire to boil their pottage,
Two poor old Dames, as I have known,
Will often live in one small cottage ;
But she, poor woman ! housed alone.
'T was well enough when summer came,
The long, warm, lightsome summer day,
Then at her door the canty dame
Would sit, as any linnet gay.

But when the ice our streams did fetter,
Oh, then how her old bones would shake !
You would have said, if you had met her,
'T was a hard time for Goody Blake.
Her evenings then were dull and dead :
Sad case it was, as you may think,
For very cold to go to bed,
And then for cold not sleep a wink.

O joy for her ! whene'er in winter
The winds at night had made a rout ;
And scattered many a lusty splinter,
And many a rotten bough about.
Yet never had she, well or sick,
As every man who knew her says,
A pile beforehand, turf or stick,
Enough to warm her for three days.

Now, when the frost was past enduring,
And made her poor old bones to ache,
Could anything be more alluring
Than an old hedge to Goody Blake ?
And now and then, it must be said,
When her old bones were cold and chill,
She left her fire, or left her bed,
To seek the hedge of Harry Gill.

Now Harry he had long suspected
This trespass of old Goody Blake ;
And vowed that she should be detected —
That he on her would vengeance take ;
And oft from his warm fire he 'd go,
And to the fields his road would take ;
And there at night, in frost and snow,
He watched to seize old Goody Blake.

And once behind a rick of barley,
Thus looking out did Harry stand ;
The moon was full and shining clearly,
And crisp with frost the stubble land.
— He hears a noise — he 's all awake —
Again ? — on tiptoe down the hill
He softly creeps — 't is Goody Blake ;
She 's at the hedge of Harry Gill !

Right glad was he when he beheld her ;
Stick after stick did Goody pull :
He stood behind a bush of elder,
Till she had fill'd her apron full.
When with her load she turned about
The by-way back again to take ;
He started forward with a shout,
And sprang upon poor Goody Blake.

And fiercely by the arm he took her,
And by the arm he held her fast,
And fiercely by the arm he shook her,
And cried, 'I 've caught you then at last !'
Then Goody, who had nothing said,
Her bundle from her lap let fall,
And kneeling on the sticks she prayed
To God that is the judge of all.

She prayed, her withered hand uprearing,
While Harry held her by the arm —
'God, who art never out of hearing,
O may he never more be warm !'
The cold, cold moon above her head,
Thus on her knees did Goody pray ;
Young Harry heard what she had said,
And icy cold he turned away.

He went complaining all the morrow
That he was cold and very chill :
His face was gloom, his heart was sorrow,
Alas ! that day for Harry Gill !
That day he wore a riding-coat,
But not a whit the warmer he :
Another was on Thursday bought ;
And ere the Sabbath he had three.

'T was all in vain, a useless matter,
And blankets were about him pinned ;
Yet still his jaws and teeth they chatter,
Like a loose casement in the wind.
And Harry's flesh it fell away ;
And all who see him say 't is plain,
That, live as long as live he may,
He never will be warm again.

No word to any man he utters,
A-bed or up, to young or old ;
But ever to himself he mutters,
' Poor Harry Gill is very cold !'
A-bed or up, by night or day,
His teeth they chatter, chatter still.
Now think, ye farmers all, I pray,
Of Goody Blake and Harry Gill !

W. Wordsworth

LXXII

THE JOVIAL BEGGAR

THERE was a jovial beggar,
  He had a wooden leg
Lame from his cradle,
  And forced for to beg.
And a-begging we will go,
  Will go, will go,
And a-begging we will go.

A bag for his oatmeal,
  Another for his salt,
And a long pair of crutches,
  To show that he can halt.
And a-begging we will go,
  Will go, will go,
And a-begging we will go.

A bag for his wheat,
  Another for his rye,
And a little bottle by his side
  To drink when he's a-dry.
And a-begging we will go,
  Will go, will go,
And a-begging we will go.

Seven years I begg'd
  For my old Master Wilde,
He taught me how to beg
  When I was but a child.
And a-begging we will go,
  Will go, will go,
And a-begging we will go.

I begg'd for my master,
  And got him store of pelf,
But goodness now be praised,
  I 'm begging for myself.
And a-begging we will go,
    Will go, will go,
And a-begging we will go.

In a hollow tree
  I live, and pay no rent,
Providence provides for me,
  And I am well content.
And a-begging we will go,
    Will go, will go,
And a-begging we will go.

Of all the occupations
  A beggar's is the best,
For whenever he 's a-weary,
  He can lay him down to rest.
And a-begging we will go,
    Will go, will go,
And a-begging we will go.

I fear no plots against me,
  I live in open cell :
Then who would be a king, lads,
  When the beggar lives so well ?
And a-begging we will go,
    Will go, will go,
And a-begging we will go.

             Old Song

LXXIII

BISHOP HATTO

THE summer and autumn had been so wet,
That in winter the corn was growing yet ;
'T was a piteous sight to see all around
The grain lie rotting on the ground.

Every day the starving poor
Crowded around Bishop Hatto's door,
For he had a plentiful last year's store,
And all the neighbourhood could tell
His granaries were furnish'd well.

At last Bishop Hatto appointed a day
To quiet the poor without delay ;
He bade them to his great barn repair,
And they should have food for the winter there.

Rejoiced such tidings good to hear,
The poor folk flock'd from far and near ;
The great barn was full as it could hold
Of women and children, and young and old.

Then when he saw it could hold no more,
Bishop Hatto he made fast the door ;
And while for mercy on Christ they call,
He set fire to the barn and burnt them all.

'I' faith, 't is an excellent bonfire !' quoth he,
'And the country is greatly obliged to me,
For ridding it in these times forlorn
Of rats, that only consume the corn.'

So then to his palace returned he,
And he sat down to supper merrily,
And he slept that night like an innocent man,
But Bishop Hatto never slept again.

In the morning as he enter'd the hall,
Where his picture hung against the wall,
A sweat like death all over him came,
For the rats had eaten it out of the frame.

As he look'd there came a man from the farm,
He had a countenance white with alarm ;
'My lord, I open'd your granaries this morn,
And the rats had eaten all your corn.'

Another came running presently,
And he was pale as pale could be,
'Fly ! my Lord Bishop, fly,' quoth he,
'Ten thousand rats are coming this way —
The Lord forgive you for yesterday !'

'I 'll go to my tower on the Rhine,' replied he,
''T is the safest place in Germany ;
The walls are high, and the shores are steep,
And the stream is strong, and the water deep.'

Bishop Hatto fearfully hasten'd away,
And he cross'd the Rhine without delay,
And reach'd his tower, and·barr'd with care
All the windows, doors, and loopholes there.

He laid him down and closed his eyes,
But soon a scream made him arise ;
He started, and saw two eyes of flame
On his pillow from whence the screaming came.

He listen'd and look'd ; it was only the cat ;
But the bishop he grew more fearful for that,
For she sat screaming, mad with fear,
At the army of rats that was drawing near.

For they have swum over the river so deep,
And they have climb'd the shores so steep,
And up the tower their way is bent
To do the work for which they were sent.

They are not to be told by the dozen or score,
By thousands they come, and by myriads and more ;
Such numbers had never been heard of before,
Such a judgment had never been witness'd of yore.

Down on his knees the bishop fell,
And faster and faster his beads did he tell,
As louder and louder drawing near
The gnawing of their teeth he could hear.

And in at the windows, and in at the door,
And through the walls helter-skelter they pour,
And down from the ceiling, and up through the floor,
From the right and the left, from behind and before,
From within and without, from above and below,
And all at once to the Bishop they go.

They have whetted their teeth against the stones,
And now they pick the Bishop's bones ;
They gnaw'd the flesh from every limb,
For they were sent to do judgment on him.

R. Southey

LXXIV

THE OLD COURTIER

A N old song made by an aged old pate,
　　Of an old worshipful gentleman who had a great
　　　estate,
That kept a brave old house at a bountiful rate,
And an old porter to relieve the poor at his gate ;
　　　　　Like an old courtier of the queen's,
　　　　　And the queen's old courtier.

With an old lady whose anger one word assuages ;
They every quarter paid their old servants their wages,
And never knew what belong'd to coachman, foot-
　　　man, nor pages,
But kept twenty old fellows with blue coats and
　　　badges ;
　　　　　Like an old courtier of the queen's,
　　　　　And the queen's old courtier.

With an old study fill'd full of learned old books,
With an old reverend chaplain, you might know him
　　　by his looks,
With an old buttery hatch worn quite off the hooks,
And an old kitchen, that maintain'd half a dozen old
　　　cooks ;
　　　　　Like an old courtier of the queen's,
　　　　　And the queen's old courtier.

With an old hall hung about with pikes, guns, and
　　　bows,
With old swords, and bucklers, that had borne many
　　　shrewd blows,

And an old frieze coat to cover his worship's trunk
    hose,
And a cup of old sherry to comfort his copper nose ;
        Like an old courtier of the queen's,
        And the queen's old courtier.

With a good old fashion when Christmas was come
To call in all his old neighbours with bagpipe and
    drum,
With a good cheer enough to furnish every old room,
And old liquor able to make a cat speak, and man
    dumb ;
        Like an old courtier of the queen's,
        And the queen's old courtier.

With an old falconer, huntsman, and a kennel of
    hounds,
That never hawk'd nor hunted but in his own grounds,
Who like a wise man kept himself within his own
    bounds,
And when he died gave every child a thousand good
    pounds ;
        Like an old courtier of the queen's,
        And the queen's old courtier.

Old Song

LXXV

JOHN GILPIN

JOHN GILPIN was a citizen
 Of credit and renown,
A train-band captain eke was he
 Of famous London Town.

John Gilpin's spouse said to her dear,
 'Though wedded we have been
These twice ten tedious years, yet we
 No holiday have seen.

'To-morrow is our wedding-day,
 And we will then repair
Unto the Bell at Edmonton,
 All in a chaise and pair.

'My sister and my sister's child,
 Myself, and children three,
Will fill the chaise ; so you must ride
 On horseback after we.'

He soon replied, 'I do admire
 Of womankind but one,
And you are she, my dearest dear,
 Therefore it shall be done.

'I am a linen-draper bold,
 As all·the world doth know,
And my good friend, the Calender,
 Will lend his horse to go.'

Quoth Mrs. Gilpin, ' That 's well said ;
　And for that wine is dear,
We will be furnish'd with our own,
　Which is both bright and clear.'

John Gilpin kiss'd his loving wife ;
　O'erjoy'd was he to find
That, though on pleasure she was bent,
　She had a frugal mind.

The morning came, the chaise was brought,
　But yet was not allowed
To drive up to the door, lest all
　Should say that she was proud.

So three doors off the chaise was stay'd,
　Where they did all get in,
Six precious souls, and all agog
　To dash through thick and thin.

Smack went the whip, round went the wheels,
　Were never folk so glad ;
The stones did rattle underneath,
　As if Cheapside were mad.

John Gilpin, at his horse's side,
　Seiz'd fast the flowing mane,
And up he got, in haste to ride,
　But soon came down again.

For saddle-tree scarce reach'd had he,
　His journey to begin,
When, turning round his head, he saw
　Three customers come in.

So down he came ; for loss of time,
  Although it grieved him sore,
Yet loss of pence, full well he knew,
  Would trouble him much more.

'T was long before the customers
  Were suited to their mind,
When Betty, screaming, came down-stairs,
  ' The wine is left behind ! '

' Good lack ! ' quoth he, ' yet bring it me,
  My leathern belt likewise,
In which I bear my trusty sword
  When I do exercise.'

Now mistress Gilpin, (careful soul!)
  Had two stone-bottles found,
To hold the liquor that she loved,
  And keep it safe and sound.

Each bottle had a curling ear,
  Through which the belt he drew,
And hung a bottle on each side,
  To make his balance true.

Then over all, that he might be
  Equipp'd from top to toe,
His long red cloak, well brush'd and neat,
  He manfully did throw.

Now see him mounted once again
  Upon his nimble steed,
Full slowly pacing o'er the stones,
  With caution and good heed.

But finding soon a smoother road
    Beneath his well-shod feet,
The snorting beast began to trot,
    Which gall'd him in his seat.

So, 'Fair and softly,' John he cried,
    But John he cried in vain ;
That trot became a gallop soon,
    In spite of curb and rein.

So stooping down, as needs he must
    Who cannot sit upright,
He grasp'd the mane with both his hands,
    And eke with all his might.

His horse, who never in that sort
    Had handled been before,
What thing upon his back had got
    Did wonder more and more.

Away went Gilpin, neck or nought ;
    Away went hat and wig ;
He little dreamt, when he set out,
    Of running such a rig.

The wind did blow, the cloak did fly,
    Like streamer long and gay,
Till loop and button failing both,
    At last it flew away.

Then might all people well discern
    The bottles he had slung ;
A bottle swinging at each side,
    As hath been said or sung.

10

The dogs did bark, the children scream'd,
    Up flew the windows all;
And every soul cried out, Well done!
    As loud as he could bawl.

Away went Gilpin — who but he?
    His fame soon spread around,
' He carries weight! he rides a race!
    'T is for a thousand pound!'

And still as fast as he drew near,
    'T was wonderful to view
How in a trice the turnpike men
    Their gates wide open threw.

And now, as he went bowing down
    His reeking head full low,
The bottles twain behind his back
    Were shatter'd at a blow.

Down ran the wine into the road,
    Most piteous to be seen,
Which made his horse's flanks to smoke
    As they had basted been.

But still he seem'd to carry weight,
    With leathern girdle braced;
For all might see the bottle necks
    Still dangling at his waist.

Thus all through merry Islington
    These gambols he did play,
Until he came unto the Wash
    Of Edmonton so gay;

And there he threw the wash about
  On both sides of the way,
Just like unto a trundling mop,
  Or a wild goose at play.

At Edmonton his loving wife
  From the balcony spied
Her tender husband, wondering much
  To see how he did ride.

'Stop, stop, John Gilpin ! — Here's the house' —
  They all aloud did cry ;
'The dinner waits, and we are tired' ;
  Said Gilpin, 'So am I !'

But yet his horse was not a whit
  Inclin'd to tarry there ;
For why ? his owner had a house
  Full ten miles off, at Ware.

So like an arrow swift he flew,
  Shot by an archer strong ;
So did he fly — which brings me to
  The middle of my song.

Away went Gilpin, out of breath,
  And sore against his will,
Till, at his friend the Calender's,
  His horse at last stood still.

The Calender, amazed to see
  His neighbour in such trim,
Laid down his pipe, flew to the gate,
  And thus accosted him.

'What news? what news? your tidings tell;
　Tell me you must and shall —
Say, why bare-headed you are come,
　Or why you come at all?'

Now Gilpin had a pleasant wit,
　And loved a timely joke;
And thus unto the Calender,
　In merry guise, he spoke:

'I came because your horse would come;
　And, if I well forebode,
My hat and wig will soon be here,
　They are upon the road.'

The Calender, right glad to find
　His friend in merry pin,
Return'd him not a single word,
　But to the house went in;

Whence straight he came, with hat and wig,
　A wig that flowed behind;
A hat not much the worse for wear,
　Each comely in its kind.

He held them up, and in his turn
　Thus show'd his ready wit;
'My head is twice as big as yours,
　They therefore needs must fit.

'But let me scrape the dust away,
　That hangs upon your face;
And stop and eat, for well you may
　Be in a hungry case.'

Said John, 'It is my wedding-day,
    And all the world would stare,
If wife should dine at Edmonton,
    And I should dine at Ware.'

So, turning to his horse, he said,
    'I am in haste to dine ;
'T was for your pleasure you came here,
    You shall go back for mine.'

Ah, luckless speech, and bootless boast !
    For which he paid full dear ;
For, while he spake, a braying ass
    Did sing most loud and clear ;

Whereat his horse did snort, as he
    Had heard a lion roar,
And gallop'd off with all his might,
    As he had done before.

Away went Gilpin, and away
    Went Gilpin's hat and wig ;
He lost them sooner than at first,
    For why ? — they were too big.

Now Mrs. Gilpin, when she saw
    Her husband posting down
Into the country far away,
    She pull'd out half-a-crown ;

And thus unto the youth she said,
    That drove them to the Bell,
'This shall be yours, when you bring back
    My husband safe and well.'

The youth did ride, and soon did meet
  John coming back amain ;
Whom in a trice he tried to stop,
  By catching at his rein ;

But not performing what he meant,
  And gladly would have done,
The frighted steed he frighted more,
  And made him faster run.

Away went Gilpin, and away
  Went postboy at his heels,
The postboy's horse right glad to miss
  The rumbling of the wheels.

Six gentlemen upon the road
  Thus seeing Gilpin fly,
With postboy scampering in the rear,
  They rais'd a hue and cry : —

' Stop thief ! — stop thief ! — a highwayman ! '
  Not one of them was mute ;
And all and each that passed that way
  Did join in the pursuit.

And now the turnpike gates again
  Flew open in short space :
The toll-men thinking, as before,
  That Gilpin rode a race.

And so he did, and won it too,
  For he got first to town ;
Nor stopp'd till where he had got up
  He did again get down.

Now let us sing, long live the king,
   And Gilpin, long live he ;
And, when he next doth ride abroad,
   May I be there to see.

W. Cowper

LXXVI

THE MILKMAID

O NCE on a time a rustic dame,
    (No matter for the lady's name,)
Wrapt up in deep imagination,
Indulg'd her pleasing contemplation ;
While on a bench she took her seat,
And plac'd the milk-pail at her feet.
Oft in her hand she chink'd the pence,
The profits which arose from thence ;
While fond ideas fill'd her brain
Of layings up, and monstrous gain,
Till every penny which she told
Creative fancy turn'd to gold ;
And reasoning thus from computation,
She spoke aloud her meditation.

   ' Please heaven but to preserve my health,
No doubt I shall have store of wealth ;
It must of consequence ensue
I shall have store of lovers too.
O, how I 'll break their stubborn hearts
With all the pride of female arts.
What suitors then will kneel before me !
Lords, Earls, and Viscounts shall adore me.

When in my gilded coach I ride,
My Lady, at his Lordship's side,
How will I laugh at all I meet
Clattering in pattens down the street!
And Lobbin then I 'll mind no more,
Howe'er I loved him heretofore;
Or, if he talks of plighted truth,
I will not hear the simple youth,
But rise indignant from my seat,
And spurn the lubber from my feet.'

Action, alas! the speaker's grace,
Ne'er came in more improper place,
For in the tossing forth her shoe
What fancied bliss the maid o'erthrew!
While down at once, with hideous fall,
Came lovers, wealth, and milk, and all.

R. Lloyd

LXXVII

SIR SIDNEY SMITH

GENTLEFOLKS, in my time, I 've made many a
rhyme,
But the song I now trouble you with
Lays some claim to applause, and you 'll grant it,
because
The subject 's Sir Sidney Smith, it is;
The subject 's Sir Sidney Smith.

We all know Sir Sidney, a man of such kidney,
He 'd fight every foe he could meet;

Give him one ship or two, and without more ado,
  He 'd engage if he met a whole fleet, he would ;
  He 'd engage if he met a whole fleet.

Thus he took, every day, all that came in his way,
  Till fortune, that changeable elf,
Order'd accidents so, that, while taking the foe,
  Sir Sidney got taken himself, he did ;
  Sir Sidney got taken himself.

His captors, right glad of the prize they now had,
  Rejected each offer we bid,
And swore he should stay, lock'd up till doomsday,
  But he swore he 'd be hang'd if he did, he did ;
  But he swore he 'd be hang'd if he did.

So Sir Sid got away, and his gaoler next day
  Cried, ' Sacre, diable, morbleu !
Mon prisonnier 'scape, I 'ave got in von scrape,
  And I fear I must run away, too, I must ;
  I fear I must run away too.'

T. Dibdin

LXXVIII

THE PIED PIPER OF HAMELIN

HAMELIN Town 's in Brunswick,
  By famous Hanover city ;
  The river Weser deep and wide
  Washes its walls on the southern side ;
  A pleasanter spot you never spied ;
  But, when begins my ditty,
  Almost five hundred years ago,

To see the townsfolk suffer so
   From vermin, was a pity.

  Rats !
They fought the dogs and killed the cats,
   And bit the babies in their cradles,
And ate the cheeses out of the vats,
   And licked the soup from the cook's own ladles,
Split open the kegs of salted sprats,
Made nests inside men's Sunday hats,
And even spoiled the women's chats,
     By drowning their speaking
     With shrieking and squeaking
In fifty different sharps and flats.

At last the people in a body
   To the Town-hall came flocking :
''T is clear,' cried they, 'our Mayor's a noddy :
   And as for our Corporation — shocking
   To think we buy gowns lined with ermine
   For dolts that can't or won't determine
   What's best to rid us of our vermin !
   You hope, because you're old and obese,
   To find in the furry civic robe ease !
Rouse up, Sirs ! Give your brains a racking
To find the remedy we're lacking,
Or, sure as fate, we'll send you packing !'
At this the Mayor and Corporation
Quaked with a mighty consternation.

An hour they sat in council,
   At length the Mayor broke silence :
'For a guilder I'd my ermine gown sell ;
   I wish I were a mile hence !
It's easy to bid one rack one's brain —

I 'm sure my poor head aches again,
I 've scratched it so, and all in vain.
Oh for a trap, a trap, a trap ! '
Just as he said this, what should hap
At the chamber door, but a gentle tap ?
' Bless us,' cried the Mayor, ' what 's that ?
Anything like the sound of a rat
Makes my heart go pit-a-pat !

' Come in ! ' the Mayor cried, looking bigger :
And in did come the strangest figure !
His queer long coat from heel to head
Was half of yellow, and half of red ;
And he himself was tall and thin,
With sharp blue eyes each like a pin,
And light loose hair, yet swarthy skin,
No tuft on cheek, nor beard on chin,
But lips where smiles went out and in —
There was no guessing his kith and kin !
And nobody could enough admire
The tall man and his quaint attire :
Quoth one, ' It 's as if my great-grandsire,
Starting up at the trump of Doom's tone,
Had walked this way from his painted tombstone ! '

He advanced to the council table :
And, ' Please your honours,' said he, ' I 'm able,
By means of a secret charm, to draw
All creatures living beneath the sun,
That creep, or swim, or fly, or run,
After me so as you never saw !
And I chiefly use my charm
On creatures that do people harm,
The mole, the toad, the newt, the viper ;

And people call me the Pied Piper.
Yet,' said he, ' poor piper as I am,
In Tartary I freed the Cham,
Last June, from his huge swarm of gnats ;
I eased in Asia the Nizam
Of a monstrous brood of vampyre bats :
And as for what your brain bewilders,
If I can rid your town of rats
    Will you give a thousand guilders ?'
    ' One ? fifty thousand !' was the exclamation
Of the astonished Mayor and Corporation.

Into the street the Piper stept,
    Smiling first a little smile,
As if he knew what magic slept
    In his quiet pipe the while ;
Then like a musical adept,
To blow the pipe his lips he wrinkled,
And green and blue his sharp eyes twinkled,
Like a candle flame where salt is sprinkled ;
And ere three shrill notes the pipe had uttered,
You heard as if an army muttered ;
And the muttering grew to a grumbling ;
And the grumbling grew to a mighty rumbling ;
And out of the houses the rats came tumbling —
Great rats, small rats, lean rats, brawny rats,
Brown rats, black rats, gray rats, tawny rats,
Grave old plodders, gay young friskers,
    Fathers, mothers, uncles, cousins,
Cocking tails, and pricking whiskers,
    Families by tens and dozens,
Brothers, sisters, husbands, wives —
Followed the Piper for their lives.
From street to street he piped, advancing,

And step for step they followed dancing,
Until they came to the river Weser
Wherein all plunged and perished,
Save one, who stout as Julius Cæsar,
Swam across, and lived to carry
(As *he* the manuscript he cherished)
To Rat-land home his commentary,
Which was, ' At the first shrill notes of the pipe,
I heard a sound as of scraping tripe,
And putting apples wondrous ripe
Into a cider press's gripe ;
And a moving away of pickle-tub boards,
And a leaving ajar of conserve cupboards,
And a drawing the corks of train-oil-flasks,
And a breaking the hoops of butter casks ;
And it seemed as if a voice
(Sweeter far than by harp or by psaltery
Is breathed) called out, Oh rats, rejoice !
The world is grown to one vast drysaltery !
So munch on, crunch on, take your nuncheon,
Breakfast, dinner, supper, luncheon !
And just as a bulky sugar puncheon,
All ready staved, like a great sun shone
Glorious, scarce an inch before me,
Just as methought it said, " Come, bore me ! "
— I found the Weser rolling o'er me.'

You should have heard the Hamelin people
Ringing the bells till they rocked the steeple ;
' Go,' cried the Mayor, ' and get long poles !
Poke out the nests, and block up the holes !
Consult with carpenters and builders,
And leave in our town not even a trace
Of the rats !' When suddenly up the face

Of the Piper perked in the market-place,
With a ' First, if you please, my thousand guilders ! '

A thousand guilders !   The Mayor looked blue,
So did the Corporation too.
For council dinners made rare havock
With Claret, Moselle, Vin-de-Grave, Hock ;
And half the money would replenish
Their cellar's biggest butt with Rhenish.
To pay this sum to a wandering fellow
With a gypsy coat of red and yellow !
' Besides,' quoth the Mayor, with a knowing wink,
' Our business was done at the river's brink ;
We saw with our eyes the vermin sink,
And what 's dead can 't come to life, I think.
So, friend, we 're not the folks to shrink
From the duty of giving you something for drink,
And a matter of money to put in your poke ;
But, as for the guilders, what we spoke
Of them, as you very well know, was in joke —
Beside, our losses have made us thrifty :
A thousand guilders ! come, take fifty ! '

The Piper's face fell, and he cried,
' No trifling !   I can't wait beside !
I 've promised to visit by dinner-time
Bagdat, and accept the prime
Of the head-cook's pottage, all he 's rich in,
For having left in the caliph's kitchen,
Of a nest of scorpions no survivor.
With him I proved no bargain-driver,
With you, don't think I 'll bate a stiver !
And folks who put me in a passion
May find me pipe to another fashion.'

' How ? ' cried the Mayor, ' d'ye think I'll brook
Being worse treated than a cook ?
Insulted by a lazy ribald
With idle pipe and vesture piebald ?
You threaten us, fellow ?   Do your worst,
Blow your pipe there till you burst.'

Once more he stept into the street,
    And to his lips again
Laid his long pipe of smooth, straight cane ;
    And ere he blew three notes (such sweet
Soft notes as yet musician's cunning
    Never gave the enraptured air),
There was a rustling that seemed like a bustling,
Of merry crowds justling at pitching and hustling,
Small feet were pattering, wooden shoes clattering,
Little hands clapping and little tongues chattering,
And like fowls in a farmyard when barley is scattering
Out came the children running :
All the little boys and girls,
With rosy cheeks and flaxen curls,
And sparkling eyes and teeth like pearls,
Tripping and skipping ran merrily after
The wonderful music with shouting and laughter.

The Mayor was dumb, and the Council stood
As if they were changed into blocks of wood,
Unable to move a step, or cry
To the children merrily skipping by —
And could only follow with the eye
That joyous crowd at the Piper's back.
And now the Mayor was on the rack,
And the wretched Council's bosoms beat,
As the Piper turned from the High Street

To where the Weser rolled its waters
Right in the way of their sons and daughters !
However he turned from south to west,
And to Koppelberg Hill his steps addressed,
And after him the children pressed ;
Great was the joy in every breast.
' He never can cross that mighty top ;
He 's forced to let the piping drop,
And we shall see our children stop ! '
When, lo ! as they reached the mountain's side,
A wondrous portal opened wide,
As if a cavern was suddenly hollowed ;
And the Piper advanced, and the children followed,
And when all were in to the very last,
The door in the mountain side shut fast.
Did I say, all ?   No !   One was lame,
And could not dance the whole of the way ;
And in after years, if you would blame
His sadness, he was used to say, —
' It 's dull in our town since my playmates left !
I can't forget that I 'm bereft
Of all the pleasant sights they see,
Which the Piper also promised me :
For he led us, he said, to a joyous land,
Joining the town and just at hand,
Where waters gushed and fruit-trees grew,
And flowers put forth a fairer hue,
And everything was strange and new ;
The sparrows were brighter than peacocks here,
And their dogs outran our fallow-deer,
And honey-bees had lost their stings,
And horses were born with eagles' wings ;
And just as I became assured
My lame foot would be speedily cured,

The music stopped and I stood still,
And found myself outside the hill,
Left alone against my will,
To go now limping as before,
And never hear of that country more!'

The Mayor sent east, west, north, and south
To offer the Piper by word of mouth,
   Wherever it was man's lot to find him,
Silver and gold to his heart's content,
If he'd only return the way he went,
   And bring the children behind him.
But when they saw 't was a lost endeavour,
And Piper and dancers were gone for ever,
They made a decree that lawyers never
   Should think their records dated duly,
If after the day of the month and year
These words did not as well appear,
   'And so long after what happened here
   On the twenty-second of July,
Thirteen hundred and seventy-six':
And the better in memory to fix
The place of the children's last retreat,
They called it, the Pied Piper's Street —
Where any one playing on pipe or tabor,
Was sure for the future to lose his labour.
Nor suffered they hostelry or tavern
   To shock with mirth a street so solemn;
But opposite the place of the cavern
   They wrote the story on a column,
And on the great church window painted
The same, to make the world acquainted
How their children were stolen away;
And there it stands to this very day.

11

And I must not omit to say
That in Transylvania there 's a tribe
Of alien people, that ascribe
The outlandish ways and dress
On which their neighbours lay such stress,
To their fathers and mothers having risen
Out of some subterraneous prison
Into which they were trepanned
Long ago in a mighty band,
Out of Hamelin town in Brunswick land,
But how or why, they don't understand.

So Willy, let you and me be wipers
Of scores out with all men, — especially pipers,
And whether they pipe us free from rats or from mice
If we 've promised them aught, let us keep our promise.

R. Browning

LXXIX

THE TIGER

TIGER, tiger, burning bright
In the forest of the night !
What immortal hand or eye
Could frame thy fearful symmetry ?

In what distant deeps or skies
Burnt the ardour of thine eyes?
On what wings dare he aspire —
What the hand dare seize the fire ?

And what shoulder, and what art
Could twist the sinews of thy heart ?

And when thy heart began to beat,
What dread hand form'd thy dread feet?

What the hammer, what the chain,
In what furnace was thy brain?
Did God smile his work to see?
Did He who made the lamb make thee?

                                        W. Blake

LXXX

KING JOHN AND THE ABBOT OF CANTERBURY

AN ancient story I'll tell you anon
  Of a notable prince, that was called King John;
And he ruled England with main and with might,
For he did great wrong and maintain'd little right.

And I'll tell you a story, a story so merry,
Concerning the Abbot of Canterbury;
How for his housekeeping and high renown,
They rode post for him to fair London town.

An hundred men, the king did hear say,
The Abbot kept in his house every day;
And fifty gold chains, without any doubt,
In velvet coats waited the Abbot about.

'How now, father Abbot, I hear it of thee,
Thou keepest a far better house than me;
And for thy housekeeping and high renown,
I fear thou work'st treason against my crown.'

'My liege,' quoth the Abbot, 'I would it were known
I never spend nothing but what is my own ;
And I trust your grace will do me no deere
For spending of my own true gotten geere.'

Yes, yes, father Abbot, thy fault it is high,
And now for the same thou needest must die ;
For except thou canst answer me questions three,
Thy head shall be smitten from thy bodie.

'And first,' quoth the king, 'when I 'm in this stead,
With my crown of gold so fair on my head,
Among all my liege-men so noble of birth,
Thou must tell me to one penny what I am worth.

'Secondly tell me, without any doubt,
How soon I may ride the whole world about ;
And at the third question thou must not shrink,
But tell me here truly what I do think.'

'O these are hard questions for my shallow wit,
Nor I cannot answer your Grace as yet ;
But if you will give me but three weeks space,
I 'll do my endeavour to answer your Grace.'

'Now three weeks space to thee will I give,
And that is the longest time thou hast to live ;
For if thou dost not answer my questions three,
Thy lands and thy livings are forfeit to me.'

Away rode the Abbot all sad at that word,
And he rode to Cambridge and Oxenford ;
But never a doctor there was so wise,
That could with his learning an answer devise.

Then home rode the Abbot of comfort so cold,
And he met his shepherd a going to fold :
'How now, my lord Abbot, you are welcome home ;
What news do you bring us from good King John ?'

'Sad news, sad news, shepherd, I must give,
That I have but three days more to live ;
For if I do not answer him questions three,
My head will be smitten from my bodie.

'The first is to tell him there in that stead,
With his crown of gold so fair on his head,
Among all his liege-men so noble of birth,
To within one penny of what he is worth.

'The second, to tell him without any doubt,
How soon he may ride this whole world about ;
And at the third question I must not shrink,
But tell him there truly what he does think.'

'Now cheer up, sir Abbot, did you never hear yet
That a fool he may learn a wise man wit ?
Lend me horse, and serving men, and your apparel,
And I 'll ride to London to answer your quarrel.

'Nay, frown not, if it hath been told unto me,
I am like your lordship as ever may be ;
And if you will but lend me your gown
There is none shall know us in fair London town.'

'Now horses and serving men thou shalt have,
With sumptuous array most gallant and brave,
With crozier, and mitre, and rochet, and cope,
Fit to appear 'fore our father the Pope.'

' Now welcome, sir Abbot,' the king he did say,
' 'T is well thou 'rt come back to keep thy day :
For and if thou canst answer my questions three,
Thy life and thy living both saved shall be.

' And first, when thou seest me here in this stead,
With my crown of gold so fair on my head,
Among all my liege-men so noble of birth,
Tell me to one penny what I am worth.'

' For thirty pence our Saviour was sold
Among the false Jews, as I have been told :
And twenty-nine is the worth of thee,
For I think thou art one penny worser than he.'

The King he laugh'd, and swore by St. Bittel,
' I did not think I had been worth so little !
Now secondly tell me, without any doubt,
How soon I may ride this whole world about.'

' You must rise with the sun, and ride with the same,
Until the next morning he riseth again ;
And then your Grace need not make any doubt
But in twenty-four hours you 'll ride it about.'

The King he laugh'd, and swore by St. Jone,
' I did not think it could be gone so soon.
Now from the third question thou must not shrink,
But tell me here truly what I do think.'

' Yea, that I shall do and make your Grace merry ;
You think I 'm the Abbot of Canterbury ;
But I 'm his poor shepherd, as plain you may see,
That am come to beg pardon for him and for me.'

The King he laugh'd, and swore by the mass,
'I 'll make thee lord abbot this day in his place !'
'Nay, nay, my liege, be not in such speed,
For alack, I can neither write nor read.'

'Four nobles a week, then, I will give thee,
For this merry jest thou hast shown unto me ;
And tell the old Abbot, when thou com'st home,
Thou hast brought him a pardon from good King
  John.'

Old Ballad

LXXXI

THE FAIRIES

UP the airy mountain,
    Down the rushy glen,
We dare n't go a-hunting
    For fear of little men ;
Wee folk, good folk,
    Trooping all together ;
Green jacket, red cap,
    And white owl's feather !

Down along the rocky shore
    Some make their home,
They live on crispy pancakes
    Of yellow tide-foam ;
Some in the reeds
    Of the black mountain lake,
With frogs for their watch-dogs,
    All night awake.

High on the hill-top
　The old king sits ;
He is now so old and gray
　He 's nigh lost his wits.
With a bridge of white mist
　Columbkill he crosses,
On his stately journeys
　From Slieveleague to Rosses ;
Or going up with music
　On cold starry nights,
To sup with the queen
　Of the gay Northern Lights.

They stole little Bridget
　For seven years long ;
When she came down again,
　Her friends were all gone.
They took her lightly back,
　Between the night and morrow,
They thought that she was fast asleep,
　But she was dead with sorrow.
They have kept her ever since
　Deep within the lakes,
On a bed of flag leaves,
　Watching till she wakes.

By the craggy hill-side,
　Through the mosses bare
They have planted thorn-trees
　For pleasure here and there.
Is any man so daring
　As dig one up in spite,
He shall find the thornies set
　In his bed at night.

Up the airy mountain,
　Down the rushy glen,
We dare n't go a-hunting
　For fear of little men ;
Wee folk, good folk,
　Trooping all together ;
Green jacket, red cap,
　And white owl's feather !
　　　　　　W. Allingham

LXXXII

THE SUFFOLK MIRACLE

A WONDER stranger ne'er was known
　Than what I now shall treat upon.
In Suffolk there did lately dwell
A farmer rich and known full well.

He had a daughter fair and bright,
On whom he placed his chief delight ;
Her beauty was beyond compare,
She was both virtuous and fair.

There was a young man living by,
Who was so charmed with her eye,
That he could never be at rest ;
He was by love so much possest.

He made address to her, and she
Did grant him love immediately ;
But when her father came to hear,
He parted her and her poor dear.

Forty miles distant was she sent,
Unto his brothers, with intent
That she should there so long remain,
Till she had changed her mind again.

Hereat this young man sadly grieved,
But knew not how to be relieved ;
He sigh'd and sobb'd continually
That his true love he could not see.

She by no means could to him send,
Who was her heart's epoused friend ;
He sigh'd, he griev'd, but all in vain,
For she confined must still remain.

He mourn'd so much that doctor's art
Could give no ease unto his heart,
Who was so strangely terrified,
That in short time for love he died.

She that from him was sent away
Knew nothing of his dying day,
But constant still she did remain,
And loved the dead, although in vain.

After he had in grave been laid
A month or more, unto this maid
He came in middle of the night
Who joy'd to see her heart's delight.

Her father's horse which well she knew,
Her mother's hood and safeguard too,
He brought with him to testify
Her parents' order he came by.

Which when her uncle understood,
He hoped it would be for her good,
And gave consent to her straightway,
That with him she should come away.

When she was got her love behind,
They passed as swift as any wind,
That in two hours, or little more,
He brought her to her father's door.

But as they did this great haste make,
He did complain his head did ache ;
Her handkerchief she then took out,
And tied the same his head about.

And unto him she thus did say :
'Thou art as cold as any clay,
When we come home a fire we 'll have ' ;
But little dreamed he went to grave.

Soon were they at her father's door,
And after she ne'er saw him more ;
'I 'll set the horse up,' then he said,
And there he left this harmless maid.

She knocked, and straight a man he cried,
' Who 's there ? '   ' 'T is I,' she then replied ;
Who wondered much her voice to hear,
And was possest with dread and fear.

Her father he did tell, and then
He stared like an affrighted man :
Down stairs he ran, and when he see her,
Cried out, ' My child, how cam'st thou here ? '

'Pray, sir, did you not send for me
By such a messenger?' said she :
Which made his hair stand on his head,
As knowing well that he was dead.

'Where is he?' then to her he said ;
'He's in the stable,' quoth the maid.
'Go in,' said he, 'and go to bed ;
I'll see the horse well littered.'

He stared about, and there could he
No shape of any mankind see,
But found his horse all on a sweat ;
Which made him in a deadly fret.

His daughter he said nothing to,
Nor none else, (though full well they knew
That he was dead a month before,)
For fear of grieving her full sore.

Her father to the father went
Of the deceased, with full intent
To tell him what his daughter said ;
So both came back unto this maid.

They asked her, and she still did say
'Twas he that then brought her away ;
Which when they heard, they were amazed,
And on each other strangely gazed.

A handkerchief she said she tied
About his head, and that they tried ;
The sexton they did speak unto
That he the grave would then undo.

Affrighted then they did behold
His body turning into mould,
And though he had a month been dead
This handkerchief was about his head.

This thing unto her then they told,
And the whole truth they did unfold ;
She was thereat so terrified
And grieved, that she quickly died.

Old Ballad

LXXXIII

THE NIGHTINGALE

A S it fell upon a day
In the merry month of May,
Sitting in a pleasant shade
Which a grove of myrtles made,
Beasts did leap and birds did sing,
Trees did grow and plants did spring,
Everything did banish moan,
Save the Nightingale alone.
She, poor bird, as all forlorn,
Lean'd her breast against a thorn,
And there sung the dolefullest ditty
That to hear it was great pity.
Fie, fie, fie, now would she cry ;
Tereu, Tereu, by and by :
That to hear her so complain
Scarce I could from tears refrain ;
For her griefs so lively shown
Made me think upon mine own.

— Ah, thought I, thou mourn'st in vain,
None takes pity on thy pain :
Senseless trees, they cannot hear thee,
Ruthless beasts, they will not cheer thee ;
King Pandion, he is dead,
All thy friends are lapp'd in lead.
All thy fellow birds do sing
Careless of thy sorrowing.
Even so, poor bird, like thee
None alive will pity me.

R. Barnefield

LXXXIV

ON A FAVOURITE CAT DROWNED IN A TUB OF GOLDFISHES

'TWAS on a lofty vase's side
  Where China's gayest art had dyed
 The azure flowers that blow,
Demurest of the tabby kind,
The pensive Selima, reclined,
 Gazed on the lake below.

Her conscious tail her joy declared :
The fair round face, the snowy beard,
 The velvet of her paws,
Her coat that with the tortoise vies,
Her eyes of jet. and emerald eyes,
 She saw, and purr'd applause.

Still had she gazed, but midst the tide
Two angel forms were seen to glide,

The genii of the stream :
Their scaly armour's Tyrian hue,
Through richest purple, to the view
   Betray'd a golden gleam.

The hapless Nymph with wonder saw :
A whisker first, and then a claw,
   With many an ardent wish,
She stretch'd in vain to reach the prize ;
What female heart can gold despise ?
   What cat 's averse to fish ?

Presumptuous maid ! with looks intent
Again she stretch'd, again she bent,
   Nor knew the gulf between —
Malignant fate sat by and smiled —
The slippery verge her feet beguiled ;
   She tumbled headlong in !

Eight times emerging from the flood
She mew'd to every watery god
   Some speedy aid to send :
No dolphin came, no Nereid stirr'd,
Nor cruel Tom nor Susan heard —
   A favourite has no friend !

               T. Gray

LXXXV

THE FOX AT THE POINT OF DEATH

A FOX, in life's extreme decay,
 Weak, sick and faint, expiring lay;
All appetite had left his maw,
And age disarm'd his mumbling jaw.
His numerous race around him stand
To learn their dying sire's command:
He rais'd his head with whining moan,
And thus was heard the feeble tone:

 'Ah, sons, from evil ways depart;
My crimes lie heavy on my heart.
See, see, the murder'd geese appear!
Why are those bleeding turkeys there?
Why all around this cackling train
Who haunt my ears for chickens slain?'

 The hungry foxes round them star'd,
And for the promised feast prepar'd.

 'Where, sir, is all this dainty cheer?
Nor turkey, goose, nor hen is here.
These are the phantoms of your brain;
And your sons lick their lips in vain.'

 'O, gluttons,' says the drooping sire,
'Restrain inordinate desire,
Your liquorish taste you shall deplore,
When peace of conscience is no more.
Does not the hound betray our pace,
And gins and guns destroy our race?
Thieves dread the searching eye of power
And never feel the quiet hour.
Old age (which few of us shall know)
Now puts a period to my woe.

Would you true happiness attain,
Let honesty your passions rein ;
So live in credit and esteem,
And the good name you lost, redeem.'
　'The counsel 's good,' a son replies,
'Could we perform what you advise.
Think what our ancestors have done ;
A line of thieves from son to son.
To us descends the long disgrace,
And infamy hath marked our race.
Though we like harmless sheep should feed,
Honest in thought, in word, in deed,
Whatever hen-roost is decreas'd,
We shall be thought to share the feast.
The change shall never be believ'd,
A lost good name is ne'er retriev'd.'
　'Nay then,' replies the feeble fox,
'(But hark, I hear a hen that clucks,)
Go ; but be moderate in your food ;
A chicken, too, might do me good.'

　　　　　　　　　　　J. Gay

LXXXVI

THE OLD MAN'S COMFORTS, AND HOW HE GAINED THEM

'YOU are old, Father William,' the young man
　　　cried,
　'The few locks which are left you are gray ;
You are hale, Father William, a hearty old man,
　Now tell me the reason, I pray.'

12

'In the days of my youth,' Father William replied,
'I remember'd that youth would fly fast,
And abused not my health and my vigour at first,
That I never might need them at last.'

'You are old, Father William,' the young man cried,
'And pleasures with youth pass away;
And yet you lament not the days that are gone,
Now tell me the reason, I pray.'

'In the days of my youth,' Father William replied,
'I remember'd that youth could not last;
I thought of the future whatever I did,
That I never might grieve for the past.'

'You are old, Father William,' the young man cried,
'And life must be hastening away;
You are cheerful, and love to converse upon death,
Now tell me the reason, I pray.'

'I am cheerful, young man,' Father William replied,
'Let the cause thy attention engage;
In the days of my youth I remember'd my God,
And He hath not forgotten my age.'

R. Southey

LXXXVII

THE CHARGE OF THE LIGHT BRIGADE

I

HALF a league, half a league,
　　Half a league onward,
All in the valley of Death
　　Rode the six hundred.
'Forward, the Light Brigade!
Charge for the guns!' he said:
Into the valley of Death
　　Rode the six hundred.

2

'Forward, the Light Brigade!'
Was there a man dismay'd?
Not though the soldier knew
　　Some one had blunder'd.
Theirs not to make reply,
Theirs not to reason why,
Theirs but to do and die.
Into the valley of Death
　　Rode the six hundred.

3

Cannon to right of them,
Cannon to left of them,
Cannon in front of them
　　Volley'd and thunder'd;
Storm'd at with shot and shell,
Boldly they rode and well,
Into the jaws of Death,
Into the mouth of Hell
　　Rode the six hundred.

4

Flash'd all their sabres bare,
Flash'd as they turn'd in air,
Sabring the gunners there,
Charging an army, while
    All the world wonder'd :
Plunged in the battery smoke,
Right through the line they broke ;
Cossack and Russian
Reel'd from the sabre stroke
    Shatter'd and sunder'd ;
Then they rode back, but not —
    Not the six hundred.

5

Cannon to right of them,
Cannon to left of them,
Cannon behind them
    Volley'd and thunder'd ;
Storm'd at with shot and shell,
While horse and hero fell,
They that had fought so well
Came through the jaws of Death
Back from the mouth of Hell,
All that was left of them,
    Left of six hundred.

6

When can their glory fade ?
O, the wild charge they made !
    All the world wonder'd.
Honour the charge they made !
Honour the Light Brigade,
    Noble six hundred !

                                    A. Tennyson

LXXXVIII

YE MARINERS OF ENGLAND

YE mariners of England,
　That guard our native seas ;
Whose flag has braved a thousand years
The battle and the breeze !
Your glorious standard launch again,
To match another foe !
And sweep through the deep,
While the stormy winds do blow ;
While the battle rages loud and long,
And the stormy winds do blow.

The spirits of your fathers
Shall start from every wave ! —
For the deck it was their field of fame,
And Ocean was their grave :
Where Blake and mighty Nelson fell,
Your manly hearts shall glow,
As ye sweep through the deep,
While the stormy winds do blow ;
While the battle rages loud and long,
And the stormy winds do blow.

Britannia needs no bulwarks,
No towers along the steep ;
Her march is o'er the mountain-waves,
Her home is on the deep.
With thunders from her native oak,
She quells the floods below,
As they roar on the shore,
When the stormy winds do blow ;

When the battle rages loud and long,
And the stormy winds do blow.

The meteor flag of England
Shall yet terrific burn ;
Till danger's troubled night depart,
And the star of peace return.
Then, then, ye ocean warriors !
Our song and feast shall flow
To the fame of your name,
When the storm has ceased to blow :
When the fiery fight is heard no more,
And the storm has ceased to blow.

T. Campbell

LXXXIX

NAPOLEON AND THE SAILOR

A True Story

NAPOLEON'S banners at Boulogne
   Arm'd in our island every freeman,
His navy chanced to capture one
   Poor British seaman.

They suffer'd him — I know not how —
   Unprison'd on the shore to roam ;
And aye was bent his longing brow
   On England's home.

His eye, methinks, pursued the flight
   Of birds to Britain half-way over ;
With envy *they* could reach the white
   Dear cliffs of Dover.

A stormy midnight watch, he thought,
   Than this sojourn would have been dearer,
If but the storm his vessel brought
   To England nearer.

At last, when care had banish'd sleep,
   He saw one morning — dreaming — doating,
An empty hogshead from the deep
   Come shoreward floating ;

He hid it in a cave, and wrought
   The livelong day laborious ; lurking
Until he launch'd a tiny boat
   By mighty working.

Heaven help us ! 't was a thing beyond
   Description wretched : such a wherry
Perhaps ne'er ventur'd on a pond,
   Or cross'd a ferry.

For ploughing in the salt sea-field,
   It would have made the boldest shudder ;
Untarr'd, uncompass'd, and unkeel'd,
   No sail — no rudder.

From neighboring woods he interlaced
   His sorry skiff with wattled willows ;
And thus equipp'd he would have pass'd
   The foaming billows —

But Frenchmen caught him on the beach,
   His little Argo sorely jeering ;
'Till tidings of him chanced to reach
   Napoleon's hearing.

With folded arms Napoleon stood,
　Serene alike in peace and danger ;
And in his wonted attitude,
　Address'd the stranger : —

' Rash man that wouldst yon channel pass
　On twigs and staves so rudely fashion'd ;
Thy heart with some sweet British lass
　Must be impassion'd.'

' I have no sweetheart,' said the lad ;
　' But — absent long from one another —
Great was the longing that I had
　To see my mother.'

' And so thou shalt,' Napoleon said,
　' Ye 've both my favour fairly won ;
A noble mother must have bred
　So brave a son.'

He gave the tar a piece of gold,
　And with a flag of truce commanded
He should be shipp'd to England Old,
　And safely landed.

Our sailor oft could scantly shift
　To find a dinner plain and hearty ;
But never changed the coin and gift
　Of Bonaparte.

T. Campbell

XC

BOADICEA

An Ode

WHEN the British warrior queen,
   Bleeding from the Roman rods,
Sought, with an indignant mien,
   Counsel of her country's gods;

Sage beneath a spreading oak
   Sat the Druid, hoary chief;
Every burning word he spoke
   Full of rage, and full of grief.

Princess ! if our aged eyes
   Weep upon thy matchless wrongs,
'T is because resentment ties
   All the terrors of our tongues.

Rome shall perish — write that word
   In the blood that she has spilt;
Perish, hopeless and abhorr'd,
   Deep in ruin as in guilt.

Rome, for empire far renown'd,
   Tramples on a thousand states;
Soon her pride shall kiss the ground —
   Hark ! the Gaul is at her gates !

Other Romans shall arise,
   Heedless of a soldier's name;
Sounds, not arms, shall win the prize,
   Harmony the path to fame.

Then the progeny that springs
    From the forests of our land,
Arm'd with thunder, clad with wings,
    Shall a wider world command.

Regions Cæsar never knew
    Thy posterity shàll sway ;
Where his eagles never flew,
    None invincible as they.

Such the bard's prophetic words,
    Pregnant with celestial fire,
Bending as he swept the chords
    Of his sweet but awful lyre.

She, with all a monarch's pride,
    Felt them in her bosom glow ;
Rush'd to battle, fought, and died ;
    Dying hurl'd them at the foe ;

Ruffians, pitiless as proud,
    Heaven awards the vengence due ;
Empire is on us bestow'd,
    Shame and ruin wait for you.
                              W. Cowper

XCI

THE SOLDIER'S DREAM

OUR bugles sang truce, for the night-cloud had
    lower'd,
And the sentinel stars set their watch in the sky ;
And thousands had sunk on the ground, overpower'd,
    The weary to sleep, and the wounded to die.

When reposing that night on my pallet of straw,
    By the wolf-scaring fagot that guarded the slain,
At the dead of the night a sweet vision I saw,
    And thrice ere the morning I dreamt it again.

Methought, from the battle-field's dreadful array,
    Far, far I had roam'd on a desolate track ;
'T was autumn — and sunshine arose on the way
    To the home of my fathers, that welcomed me back.

I flew to the pleasant fields traversed so oft
    In life's morning march, when my bosom was young ;
I heard my own mountain-goats bleating aloft,
    And knew the sweet strain that the corn-reapers sung.

Then pledged we the wine-cup, and fondly I swore,
    From my home and my weeping friends never to part,
My little ones kiss'd me a thousand times o'er,
    And my wife sobb'd aloud in her fulness of heart.

Stay, stay with us, — rest, thou art weary and worn !
    And fain was their war-broken soldier to stay ;
But sorrow return'd with the dawning of morn,
    And the voice in my dreaming ear melted away.

                    T. Campbell

XCII

LOVE AND GLORY

YOUNG Henry was as a brave a youth
    As ever graced a gallant story ;
And Jane was fair as lovely truth,
    She sigh'd for Love, and he for Glory !

With her his faith he meant to plight,
    And told her many a gallant story ;
Till war, their coming joys to blight,
    Call'd him away from Love to Glory !

Young Henry met the foe with pride ;
    Jane followed, fought ! ah, hapless story !
In man's attire, by Henry's side,
    She died for Love, and he for Glory.
                                        T. Dibdin

XCIII

AFTER BLENHEIM

IT was a summer evening,
    Old Kaspar's work was done,
And he before his cottage door
    Was sitting in the sun,
And by him sported on the green
His little grandchild Wilhelmine.

She saw her brother Peterkin
    Roll something large and round,
Which he beside the rivulet
    In playing there had found ;

He came to ask what he had found
That was so large and smooth and round.

Old Kasper took it from the boy
   Who stood expectant by ;
And then the old man shook his head,
   And with a natural sigh —
' 'T is some poor fellow's skull,' said he,
' Who fell in the great victory.'

' I find them in the garden,
   For there 's many here about ;
And often when I go to plough,
   The ploughshare turns them out.
For many a thousand men,' said he,
' Were slain in that great victory.'

' Now tell us what 't was all about,'
   Young Peterkin he cries :
And little Wilhelmine looks up
   With wonder-waiting eyes ;
' Now tell us all about the war,
And what they fought each other for.'

' It was the English,' Kaspar cried,
   Who put the French to rout ;
But what they fought each other for
   I could not well make out.
But every body said,' quoth he,
' That 't was a famous victory.

' My father lived at Blenheim then,
   Yon little stream hard by ;
They burnt his dwelling to the ground,
   And he was forced to fly :

So with his wife and child he fled,
Nor had he where to rest his head.

' With fire and sword the country round
 Was wasted far and wide,
And many a childing mother then
 And new-born baby died :
But things like that, you know, must be
At every famous victory.

' They say it was a shocking sight
 After the field was won ;
For many a thousand bodies here
 Lay rotting in the sun ;
But things like that, you know, must be
After a famous victory.

' Great praise the Duke of Marlbro' won,
 And our good Prince Eugene ' ;
' Why 't was a very wicked thing ! '
 Said little Wilhelmine ;
' Nay, nay, my little girl,' quoth he,
' It was a famous victory.

' And every body praised the Duke
 Who this great fight did win.'
' But what good came of it at last ? '
 Quoth little Peterkin.
' Why that I cannot tell,' said he,
' But 't was a famous victory.'

      R. Southey

XCIV

THE SAILOR'S MOTHER

ONE morning (raw it was and wet —
    A foggy day in winter time)
A woman on the road I met,
Not old, though something past her prime :
Majestic in her person, tall and straight ;
And like a Roman matron's was her mien and gait.

The ancient spirit is not dead ;
    Old times, thought I, are breathing there ;
Proud was I that my country bred
    Such strength, a dignity so fair :
She begged an alms like one in poor estate ;
I looked at her again, nor did my pride abate.

When from these lofty thoughts I woke,
    'What is it ?' said I, 'that you bear
Beneath the covert of your cloak,
    Protected from this cold damp air ?'
She answered, soon as she the question heard,
'A simple burthen, Sir, a little singing bird.'

And, thus continuing, she said,
    'I had a son, who many a day
Sail'd on the seas, but he is dead ;
    In Denmark he was cast away :
And I have travelled weary miles to see
If aught that he had owned might still remain for me.

The bird and cage they both were his :
    'T was my son's bird ; and neat and trim

He kept it : many voyages
The singing bird had gone with him ;
When last he sailed, he left the bird behind ;
From bodings, as might be, that hung upon his mind.'

W. Wordsworth

XCV

MAHMOUD

THERE came a man, making his hasty moan
  Before the Sultan Mahmoud on his throne,
And crying out — ' My sorrow is my right,
And I *will* see the Sultan, and to-night.'

' Sorrow,' said Mahmoud, ' is a reverend thing :
I recognize its right as king with king ;
Speak on.'   ' A fiend has got into my house,'
Exclaim'd the staring man, ' and tortures us :
One of thine officers ; — he comes, the abhorr'd,
And takes possession of my house, my board,
My bed : — I have two daughters and a wife,
And the wild villain comes and makes me mad with
    life.'

' Is he there now ?' said Mahmoud.   ' No, he left
The house when I did, of my wits bereft ;
And laugh'd me down the street because I vow'd
I 'd bring the prince himself to lay him in his shroud.
I 'm mad with want, I 'm mad with misery,
And Oh, thou Sultan Mahmoud, God cries out for
    thee !'

The Sultan comforted the man and said,
'Go home, and I will send thee wine and bread,
(For he was poor,) and other comforts.   Go ;
And should the wretch return let Sultan Mahmoud
   know.'

In two days' time, with haggard eyes and beard,
And shaken voice, the suitor re-appeared,
And said, 'He's come.' — Mahmoud said not a word,
But rose and took four slaves each with a sword,
And went with the vext man.   They reach the place,
And hear a voice and see a female face,
That to the window flutter'd in affright,
'Go in,' said Mahmoud, 'and put out the light ;
But tell the females first to leave the room ;
And when the drunkard follows them, we come.

The man went in.   There was a cry, and hark !
A table falls, the window is struck dark ;
Forth rush the breathless women, and behind
With curses comes the fiend in desperate mind.
In vain : the sabres soon cut short the strife,
And chop the shrieking wretch, and drink his bloody
   life.

'Now *light* the light,' the Sultan cried aloud.
'T was done ; he took it in his hand and bow'd
Over the corpse, and look'd upon the face ;
Then turn'd and knelt beside it in the place,
And said a prayer, and from his lips there crept
Some gentle words of pleasure, and he wept.

In reverent silence the spectators wait,
Then bring him at his call both wine and meat ;

And when he had refresh'd his noble heart,
He bade his host be blest, and rose up to depart.

The man amaz'd, all mildness now and tears,
Fell at the Sultan's feet with many prayers,
And begg'd him to vouchsafe to tell his slave,
The reason first of that command he gave
About the light : then when he saw the face,
Why he knelt down ; and lastly how it was
That fare so poor as his detain'd him in the place.

The Sultan said, with much humanity,
'Since first I heard thee come, and heard thy cry,
I could not rid me of a dread that one
By whom such daring villanies were done
Must be some lord of mine, perhaps a lawless son.
Whoe'er he was, I knew my task, but fear'd
A father's heart, in case the worst appear'd.
For this I had the light put out.   But when
I saw the face and found a stranger slain,
I knelt and thank'd the sovereign arbiter,
Whose work I had perform'd through pain and fear.
And then I rose and was refresh'd with food,
The first time since thou cam'st and marr'dst my soli-
    tude.'

L. Hunt

XCVI

AUTUMN

A Dirge

THE warm sun is failing, the bleak wind is wailing,
The bare boughs are sighing, the pale flowers are
dying ;
And the year
On the earth, her death-bed, in a shroud of leaves dead
Is lying.
Come, Months, come away,
From November to May,
In your saddest array, —
Follow the bier
Of the dead cold year,
And like dim shadows watch by her sepulchre.

The chill rain is falling, the nipt worm is crawling,
The rivers are swelling, the thunder is knelling
For the year ;
The blithe swallows are flown, and the lizards each
gone
To his dwelling.
Come, Months, come away ;
Put on white, black, and gray ;
Let your light sisters play ;
Ye, follow the bier
Of the dead cold year,
And make her grave green with tear on tear.

P. B. Shelley

XCVII

THE RAVEN

ONCE upon a midnight dreary, while I pondered, weak and weary,

Over many a quaint and curious volume of forgotten lore,

While I nodded, nearly napping, suddenly there came a tapping

As of some one gently rapping, rapping at my chamber door.

''T is some visitor,' I mutter'd, 'tapping at my chamber door —

Only this and nothing more.'

Ah, distinctly I remember it was in the bleak December,

And each separate dying ember wrought its ghost upon the floor.

Eagerly I wish'd the morrow ; — vainly had I sought to borrow

From my books surcease of sorrow, sorrow for the lost Lenore —

For the rare and radiant maiden whom the angels name Lenore —

Nameless here for evermore.

And the silken sad uncertain rustling of each purple curtain

Thrill'd me — filled me with fantastic terrors never felt before ;

So that now to still the beating of my heart, I stood repeating,

''T is some visitor entreating entrance at my chamber
     door —
Some late visitor entreating entrance at my chamber
     door ; —
       This it is, and nothing more.'

Presently my soul grew stronger; hesitating then no
     longer,
' Sir,' said I, ' or madam, truly your forgiveness I im-
     plore ;
But the fact is I was napping, and so gently you came
     rapping,
And so faintly you came tapping, tapping at my cham-
     ber door,
That I scarce was sure I heard you '; here I open'd
     wide the door ; —
       Darkness there, and nothing more.

Deep into that darkness peering, long I stood there
     wondering, fearing,
Doubting, dreaming dreams no mortal ever dared to
     dream before ;
But the silence was unbroken, and the darkness gave
     no token,
And the only word there spoken was the whisper'd
     word ' Lenore !'
This I whisper'd, and an echo murmur'd back the word
     ' Lenore ' —
       Merely this, and nothing more.

Back into the chamber turning, all my soul within me
     burning,
Soon I heard again a tapping somewhat louder than
     before.

'Surely,' said I, 'surely that is something at my window lattice;
Let me see then what thereat is, and this mystery explore —
Let my heart be still a moment and this mystery explore; —
    'T is the wind, and nothing more!'

Open here I flung a shutter, when with many a flirt and flutter
In there stepp'd a stately raven of the saintly days of yore;
Not the least obeisance made he; not an instant stopp'd or stay'd he;
But with mien of lord or lady, perch'd above my chamber door —
Perch'd upon a bust of Pallas, just above my chamber door —
    Perch'd and sat and nothing more.

Then this ebony bird beguiling my sad fancy into smiling,
By the grave and stern decorum of the countenance it wore,
'Though thy crest be shorn and shaven, thou,' I said, 'art sure no craven,
Ghastly, grim, and ancient raven wandering from the nightly shore,
Tell me what thy lordly name is on the night's Plutonian shore.'
    Quoth the raven, 'Nevermore!'

Much I marvell'd this ungainly fowl to hear discourse so plainly,

Though its answer little meaning — little relevancy
    bore ;
For we cannot help agreeing that no living human
    being
'Ever yet was blest with seeing bird above his chamber
    door,
Bird or beast upon the sculptur'd bust above his cham-
    ber door,
       With such a name as ' Nevermore.'

But the raven, sitting lonely on the placid bust, spoke
    only
That one word, as if his soul in that one word he did
    outpour ;
Nothing farther then he utter'd — not a feather then he
    flutter'd —
Till I scarcely more than mutter'd, ' Other friends have
    flown before —
On the morrow he will leave me, as my hopes have
    flown before.'
       Then the bird said, ' Nevermore.'

Startled at the stillness broken by reply so aptly
    spoken,
' Doubtless,' said I, ' what it utters is its only stock
    and store,
Caught from some unhappy master whom unmerciful
    disaster
Follow'd fast and follow'd faster, till his songs one
    burden bore —
Till the dirges of his hope that melancholy burden
    bore
       Of ' Never — nevermore.'

But the raven still beguiling all my sad soul into
smiling,
Straight I wheel'd a cushion'd seat in front of bird, and
bust, and door ;
Then, upon the velvet sinking, I betook myself to
linking
Fancy unto fancy, thinking what this ominous bird of
yore —
What this grim, ungainly, ghastly, gaunt and ominous
bird of yore
Meant in croaking ' Nevermore.'

This I sat engaged in guessing, but no syllable ex-
pressing
To the fowl whose fiery eyes now burnt into my bosom's core ;
This and more I sat divining, with my head at ease
reclining
On the cushion's velvet lining that the lamp-light
gloated o'er,
But whose velvet violet lining, with the lamp-light
gloating o'er,
She shall press, ah, nevermore !

' Prophet !' said I, ' thing of evil — prophet still, if
bird or devil !
By that heaven that bends above us, by that God we
both adore —
Tell this soul, with sorrow laden, if within the distant
Aidenn
It shall clasp a sainted maiden whom the angels name
Lenore —
Clasp a rare and radiant maiden whom the angels name
Lenore.'
Quoth the raven, ' Nevermore.'

'Be that word our sign of parting, bird or fiend!' I
　　shriek'd, upstarting —
'Get thee back into the tempest and the night's Pluto-
　　nian shore!
Leave no black plume as a token of the lie thy soul
　　hath spoken!
Leave my loneliness unbroken, quit the bust above my
　　door!
Take thy beak from out my heart and take thy form
　　from off my door!'
　　　　Quoth the raven, 'Nevermore.'

And the raven never flitting, still is sitting, still is
　　sitting,
On the pallid bust of Pallas just above my chamber
　　door;
And his eyes have all the seeming of a dæmon's that is
　　dreaming,
And the lamplight o'er him streaming throws his
　　shadow on the floor;
And my soul from out that shadow that is floating on
　　the floor
　　　　Shall be lifted 'Nevermore.'

　　　　　　　　　　　　　　E. A. Poe

XCVIII

THE NIX

THE crafty Nix, more false than fair,
    Whose haunt in arrowy Iser lies,
She envied me my golden hair,
    She envied me my azure eyes.

The moon with silvery ciphers traced
    The leaves, and on the waters play'd ;
She rose, she caught me round the waist,
    She said, 'Come down with me, fair maid.'

She led me to her crystal grot,
    She set me in her coral chair,
She waved her hand, and I had not
    Or azure eyes or golden hair.

Her locks of jet, her eyes of flame
    Were mine, and hers my semblance fair ;
'O make me, Nix, again the same,
    O give me back my golden hair !'

She smiles in scorn, she disappears,
    And here I sit and see no sun,
My eyes of fire are quenched in tears,
    And all my darksome locks undone.

R. Garnett

XCIX

THE SEVEN SISTERS; OR, THE SOLI-TUDE OF BINNORIE

1

SEVEN daughters had Lord Archibald,
 All children of one mother :
You could not say in one short day
What love they bore each other.
A garland, of seven lilies wrought !
Seven sisters that together dwell ;
But he, bold knight as ever fought,
Their father, took of them no thought,
He loved the wars so well.
Sing mournfully, oh ! mournfully,
The solitude of Binnorie !

2

Fresh blows the wind, a western wind,
And from the shores of Erin,
Across the wave, a rover brave
To Binnorie is steering :
Right onward to the Scottish strand
The gallant ship is borne ;
The warriors leap upon the land,
And hark ! the leader of the band
Hath blown his bugle horn.
Sing mournfully, oh ! mournfully,
The solitude of Binnorie !

3

Beside a grotto of their own,
With boughs above them closing,

The seven are laid, and in the shade
They lie like fawns reposing.
But now upstarting with affright
At noise of man and steed,
Away they fly, to left, to right —
Of your fair household, father-knight,
Methinks you take small heed !
Sing mournfully, oh ! mournfully,
The solitude of Binnorie !

4

Away the seven fair Campbells fly ;
And, over hill and hollow,
With menace proud, and insult loud,
The youthful rovers follow.
Cried they, ' Your father loves to roam :
Enough for him to find
The empty house when he comes home ;
For us your yellow ringlets comb,
For us be fair and kind ! '
Sing mournfully, oh ! mournfully,
The solitude of Binnorie !

5

Some close behind, some side by side,
Like clouds in stormy weather,
They run and cry, ' Nay, let us die,
And let us die together.'
A lake was near ; the shore was steep ;
There foot had never been ;
They ran, and with a desperate leap
Together plunged into the deep,
Nor ever more were seen.
Sing mournfully, oh ! mournfully,
The solitude of Binnorie !

6

The stream that flows out of the lake,
As through the glen it rambles,
Repeats a moan o'er moss and stone
For those seven lovely Campbells.
Seven little islands, green and bare,
Have risen from out the deep :
The fishers say those sisters fair
By fairies are all buried there,
And there together sleep.
Sing mournfully, oh ! mournfully,
The solitude of Binnorie !

W. Wordsworth

c

THE BEGGAR MAID

HER arms across her breast she laid ;
   She was more fair than words can say ;
Barefooted came the beggar maid
   Before the King Cophetua.
In robe and crown the king stept down,
   To meet and greet her on her way ;
'It is no wonder,' said the lords,
   'She is more beautiful than day.'

As shines the moon in clouded skies,
   She in her poor attire was seen :
One praised her ankles, one her eyes,
   One her dark hair and lovesome mien.
So sweet a face, such angel grace,
   In all that land had never been :
Cophetua swore a royal oath :
   'This beggar maid shall be my queen.'

A. Tennyson

CI

THE WILD HUNTSMAN

THE Wildgrave winds his bugle horn,
To horse, to horse ! halloo, halloo !
His fiery courser snuffs the morn,
And thronging serfs their lords pursue.

The eager pack, from couples freed,
Dash through the brush, the brier, the brake ;
While answering hound, and horn, and steed,
The mountain echoes startling wake.

The beams of God's own hallow'd day
Had painted yonder spire with gold,
And calling sinful man to pray,
Loud, long, and deep the bell had tolled.

But still the Wildgrave onward rides ;
Halloo, halloo ! and, hark again !
When spurring from opposing sides,
Two stranger horsemen join the train.

Who was each stranger, left and right,
Well may I guess but dare not tell ;
The right-hand steed was silver white,
The left, the swarthy hue of hell.

The right-hand horseman, young and fair,
His smile was like the morn of May ;
The left, from eye of tawny glare,
Shot midnight lightning's lurid ray.

He waved his huntsman's cap on high,
   Cried, ' Welcome, welcome, noble lord !
What sport can earth, or sea, or sky,
   To match the princely chase afford ? '

' Cease thy loud bugle's clanging knell,'
   Cried the fair youth with silver voice ;
' And for devotion's choral swell,
   Exchange this rude unhallow'd noise ;

' To-day the ill-omen'd chase forbear,
   Yon bell yet summons to the fane ;
To-day the warning Spirit hear,
   To-morrow thou mayst mourn in vain.'

' Away, and sweep the glades along ! '
   The sable hunter hoarse replies ;
' To muttering monks leave matin song,
   And bells, and books, and mysteries.'

The Wildgrave spurr'd his ardent steed,
   And, launching forward with a bound,
' Who, for thy drowsy priestlike rede,
   Would leave the jovial horn and hound ?

' Hence, if our manly sport offend !
   With pious fools go chant and pray ;
Well hast thou spoke, my dark-brow'd friend,
   Halloo, halloo ! and, hark away ! '

The Wildgrave spurr'd his courser light
   O'er moss and moor, o'er holt and hill ;
And on the left and on the right
   Each stranger horseman follow'd still.

Up springs from yonder tangled thorn
  A stag more white than mountain snow;
And louder rung the Wildgrave's horn,
  'Hark forward, forward! holla, ho!'

A heedless wretch has cross'd the way;
  He gasps, the thundering hoofs below;
But live who can, or die who may,
  Still 'Forward, forward!' on they go.

See, where yon simple fences meet,
  A field with autumn's blessing crown'd;
See, prostrate at the Wildgrave's feet,
  A husbandman, with toil embrown'd.

'O mercy, mercy, noble lord!
  Spare the poor's pittance,' was his cry,
'Earn'd by the sweat these brows have pour'd,
  In scorching hour of fierce July.'

Earnest the right-hand stranger pleads,
  The left still cheering to the prey;
The impetuous Earl no warning heeds,
  But furious holds the onward way.

'Away, thou hound! so basely born!
  Or dread the scourge's echoing blow!'
Then loudly rang his bugle horn,
  'Hark forward, forward, holla, ho!'

So said, so done; a single bound
  Clears the poor labourer's humble pale;
While follows man, and horse, and hound,
  Like dark December's stormy gale.

And man, and horse, and hound, and horn,
  Destructive sweep the field along ;
While, joying o'er the wasted corn,
  Fell Famine marks the maddening throng.

Again uproused, the timorous prey
  Scours moss and moor, and holt and hill ;
Hard run, he feels his strength decay,
  And trusts for life his simple skill.

Too dangerous solitude appear'd ;
  He seeks the shelter of the crowd ;
Amid the flock's domestic herd
  His harmless head he hopes to shroud.

O'er moss and moor, and holt and hill,
  His track the steady bloodhounds trace ;
O'er moss and moor, unwearied still,
  The furious Earl pursues the chase.

Full lowly did the herdsman fall ;
  ' O spare, thou noble Baron, spare
These herds, a widow's little all ;
  These flocks, an orphan's fleecy care ! '

Earnest the right-hand stranger pleads,
  The left still cheering to the prey ;
The Earl nor prayer nor pity heeds,
  But furious keeps the onward way.

' Unmanner'd dog ! To stop my sport
  Vain were thy cant and beggar whine
Though human spirits of thy sort
  Were tenants of these carrion kine ! '

14

Again he winds his bugle horn,
　' Hark forward, forward, holla, ho ! '
And through the herd in ruthless scorn
　He cheers his furious hounds to go.

In heaps the throttled victims fall ;
　Down sinks their mangled herdsman near ;
The murderous cries the stag appall, —
　Again he starts new-nerved by fear.

With blood besmear'd, and white with foam,
　While big the tears of anguish pour,
He seeks amid the forest's gloom
　The humble hermit's hallow'd bower.

But man, and horse, and horn, and hound,
　Fast rattling on his traces go ;
The sacred chapel rung around
　With ' Hark away ! and holla, ho ! '

All mild amid the rout profane,
　The holy hermit pour'd his prayer ;
' Forbear with blood God's house to stain ;
　Revere His altar, and forbear !

' The meanest brute has rights to plead,
　Which, wrong'd by cruelty or pride,
Draw vengeance on the ruthless head ; —
　Be warn'd at length, and turn aside.'

Still the Fair Horseman anxious pleads ;
　The Black, wild whooping, points the prey ;
Alas ! the Earl no warning heeds,
　But frantic keeps the forward way.

'Holy or not, or right or wrong,
   Thy altar and its rights I spurn ;
Not sainted martyrs' sainted song,
   Not God Himself shall make me turn !'

He spurs his horse, he winds his horn,
   'Hark forward, forward, holla, ho !'
But off on whirlwind's pinions borne,
   The stag, the hut, the hermit go.

And horse, and man, and horn, and hound,
   And clamour of the chase was gone ;
For hoofs, and howls, and bugle sound,
   A deadly silence reign'd alone.

Wild gazed the affrighted Earl around ;
   He strove in vain to wake his horn ;
In vain to call ; for not a sound
   Could from his anxious lips be borne.

He listens for his trusty hounds ;
   No distant baying reach'd his ears ;
His courser, rooted to the ground,
   The quickening spur unmindful bears.

Still dark and darker frown the shades,
   Dark as the darkness of the grave ;
And not a sound the still invades,
   Save what a distant torrent gave.

High o'er the sinner's humbled head
   At length the solemn silence broke ;
And from a cloud of swarthy red,
   The awful voice of thunder spoke :

'Oppressor of creation fair !
  Apostate spirits' harden'd tool !
Scorner of God, scourge of the poor !
  The measure of thy cup is full.

' Be chas'd forever through the wood :
  Forever roam the affrighted wild ;
And let thy fate instruct the proud,
  God's meanest creature is His child.'

'T was hush'd : one flash of sombre glare
  With yellow tinged the forest's brown ;
Up rose the Wildgrave's bristling hair,
  And horror chill'd each nerve and bone.

Cold pour'd the sweat in freezing rill ;
  A rising wind began to sing ;
A louder, louder, louder still,
  Brought storm and tempest on its wing.

Earth heard the call ; her entrails rend ;
  From yawning rifts, with many a yell,
Mix'd with sulphureous flames, ascend
  The misbegotten dogs of hell.

What ghastly huntsman next arose,
  Well may I guess, but dare not tell ;
His eye like midnight lightning glows,
  His steed the swarthy hue of hell.

The Wildgrave flies o'er bush and thorn,
  With many a shriek of helpless woe ;
Behind him hound, and horse, and horn ;
  And ' Hark away, and holla, ho !'

Sir W. Scott

CII

TO DAFFODILS

FAIR daffodils, we weep to see
　　You haste away so soon ;
As yet the early rising sun
　　Has not attain'd his noon :
　　　　Stay, stay,
　　Until the hastening day
　　　　Has run
　　But to the even-song ;
And having prayed together, we
　　Will go with you along.

We have short time to stay, as you ;
　　We have as short a spring :
As quick a growth to meet decay
　　As you, or any thing :
　　　　We die,
　　As your hours do ; and dry
　　　　Away
　　Like to the summer's rain,
Or as the pearls of morning dew,
　　Ne'er to be found again.
　　　　　　　　R. Herrick

CIII

THE HOMES OF ENGLAND

THE stately homes of England !
　　How beautiful they stand,
Amidst their tall ancestral trees,
　　O'er all the pleasant land !
The deer across their greensward bound
　　Through shade and sunny gleam ;
And the swan glides by them with the sound
　　Of some rejoicing stream.

The merry homes of England !
　　Around their hearths by night,
What gladsome looks of household love
　　Meet in the ruddy light !
The blessed homes of England !
　　How softly on their bowers
Is laid the holy quietness
　　That breathes from sabbath hours !

The cottage homes of England !
　　By thousands on her plains
They are smiling o'er the silvery brooks,
　　And round the hamlet fanes.
Through glowing orchards forth they peep,
　　Each from its nook of leaves ;
And fearless there the lowly sleep,
　　As the bird beneath their eaves.

The free, fair homes of England !
　　Long, long, in hut and hall,
May hearts of native proof be rear'd
　　To guard each hallow'd wall !

And green forever be the groves,
  And bright the flowery sod,
Where first the child's glad spirit loves
  Its country and its God !

F. Hemans

CIV

MARY, THE MAID OF THE INN

WHO is yonder poor maniac, whose wildly fixed
     eyes
  Seem a heart overcharged to express ?
She weeps not, yet often and deeply she sighs ;
She never complains, but her silence implies
  The composure of settled distress.

No pity she looks for, no alms doth she seek ;
  Nor for raiment nor food doth she care :
Through her tatters the winds of the winter blow bleak
On that wither'd breast, and her weather-worn cheek
  Hath the hue of a mortal despair.

Yet cheerful and happy, nor distant the day,
  Poor Mary the Maniac hath been ;
The traveller remembers who journey'd this way
No damsel so lovely, no damsel so gay,
  As Mary, the Maid of the Inn.

Her cheerful address fill'd the guests with delight
  As she welcom'd them in with a smile ;
Her heart was a stranger to childish affright,
And Mary would walk by the Abbey at night
  When the wind whistled down the dark aisle.

She loved, and young Richard had settled the day,
   And she hoped to be happy for life ;
But Richard was idle and worthless, and they
Who knew him would pity poor Mary and say
   That she was too good for his wife.

'T was in autumn, and stormy and dark was the night,
   And fast were the windows and door ;
Two guests sat enjoying the fire that burnt bright,
And, smoking in silence with tranquil delight,
   They listen'd to hear the wind roar.

' 'T is pleasant,' cried one, ' seated by the fireside
   To hear the wind whistle without.'
' What a night for the Abbey ! ' his comrade replied,
' Methinks a man's courage would now be well tried,
   Who should wander the ruins about.

' I myself, like a school-boy, should tremble to hear
   The hoarse ivy shake over my head ;
And could fancy I saw, half persuaded by fear,
Some ugly old abbot's grim spirit appear,
   For this wind might awaken the dead !'

' I 'll wager a dinner,' the other one cried,
   ' That Mary would venture there now.'
' Then wager and lose ! ' with a sneer he replied,
' I 'll warrant she 'd fancy a ghost by her side,
   And faint if she saw a white cow.'

' Will Mary this charge on her courage allow ? '
   His companion exclaimed with a smile ;
' I shall win — for I know she will venture there now
And earn a new bonnet by bringing a bough
   From the elder that grows in the aisle.'

With fearless good-humour did Mary comply,
   And her way to the Abbey she bent;
The night was dark, and the wind was high,
And as hollowly howling it swept through the sky,
   She shiver'd with cold as she went.

O'er the path so well known still proceeded the maid,
   Where the Abbey rose dim on the sight;
Through the gateway she enter'd, she felt not afraid,
Yet the ruins were lonely and wild, and their shade
   Seem'd to deepen the gloom of the night.

All around her was silent save when the rude blast
   Howl'd dismally round the old pile;
Over weed-cover'd fragments she fearlessly passed,
And arrived at the innermost ruin at last,
   Where the elder-tree grew in the aisle.

Well pleas'd did she reach it, and quickly drew near,
   And hastily gather'd the bough;
When the sound of a voice seem'd to rise on her ear,
She paus'd, and she listen'd intently, in fear,
   And her heart panted painfully now.

The wind blew, the hoarse ivy shook over her head,
   She listen'd, naught else could she hear;
The wind fell; her heart sunk in her bosom with dread,
For she heard in the ruins distinctly the tread
   Of footsteps approaching her near.

Behind a wide column half breathless with fear
   She crept to conceal herself there:
That instant the moon o'er a dark cloud shone clear,
And she saw in the moonlight two ruffians appear,
   And between them a corpse they did bear.

Then Mary could feel the heart-blood curdle cold ;
    Again the rough wind hurried by —
It blew off the hat of the one, and behold,
Even close to the feet of poor Mary it roll'd, —
    She felt, and expected to die.

'Curse the hat !' he exclaims.   'Nay, come on till we
        hide
    The dead body,' his comrade replies.
She beholds them in safety pass on by her side,
She seizes the hat, fear her courage supplied,
    And fast through the Abbey she flies.

She ran with wild speed, she rush'd in at the door,
    She gazed in her terror around,
Then her limbs could support their faint burden no
        more,
And exhausted and breathless she sank on the floor,
    Unable to utter a sound.

Ere yet her pale lips could the story impart,
    For a moment the hat met her view ;
Her eyes from that object convulsively start,
For — what a cold horror then thrill'd through her
        heart
    When the name of her Richard she knew.

Where the old Abbey stands, on the Common hard by,
    His gibbet is now to be seen ;
His irons you still from the road may espy ;
The traveller beholds them, and thinks with a sigh
    Of poor Mary, the Maid of the Inn.

                                        R. Southey

CV

THE WITCHES' MEETING

1st *Witch.*	WHEN shall we three meet again In thunder, lightning, or in rain?
2d *Witch.*	When the hurly-burley 's done, When the battle 's lost or won :
3d *Witch.*	That will be ere set of sun.
1st *Witch.*	Where the place ?
2d *Witch.*	Upon the heath ;
3d *Witch.*	There to meet with Macbeth.
1st *Witch.*	I come Grimalkin !
All.	Paddock calls : — anon — Fair is foul, and foul is fair ; Hover through the fog and filthy air.

THE CHARM

1st *Witch.*	Thrice the brinded cat hath mewed.
2d *Witch.*	Thrice : and once the hedge-pig whined.
3d *Witch.*	Harpier cries : — 'T is time, 't is time :
1st *Witch.*	Round about the caldron go : In the poison'd entrails throw. Toad, that under the cold stone, Days and nights hast thirty-one Swelter'd venom sleeping got Boil thou first i' the charmed pot !
All.	Double, double toil and trouble ; Fire burn, and, caldron, bubble.
2d *Witch.*	Fillet of a fenny snake, In the caldron boil and bake ; Eye of newt, and toe of frog, Wool of bat, and tongue of dog,

Adder's fork, and blind-worm's sting,
Lizard's leg, and owlet's wing,
For a charm of powerful trouble ;
Like a hell-broth boil and bubble.

All. Double, double toil and trouble ;
Fire burn, and, caldron, bubble.

3d Witch. Scale of dragon, tooth of wolf ;
Witches' mummy ; maw and gulf
Of the ravin'd salt sea shark ;
Root of hemlock, digged i' the dark ;
Liver of blaspheming Jew ;
Gall of goat, and slips of yew
Sliver'd in the moon's eclipse ;
Nose of Turk, and Tartar's lips ;
Add thereto a tiger's chaudron.
For the ingredients of our caldron.

All. Double, double toil and trouble ;
Fire burn, and, caldron, bubble.

2d Witch. Cool it with a baboon's blood,
Then the charm is firm and good.

W. Shakespeare

CVI

ADELGITHA

THE ordeal's fatal trumpet sounded,
  And sad pale Adelgitha came,
When forth a valiant champion bounded,
  And slew the slanderer of her fame.

She wept, deliver'd from her danger ;
  But when he knelt to claim her glove —
'Seek not,' she cried, 'oh ! gallant stranger,
  For hapless Adelgitha's love.

'For he is in a foreign far land
  Whose arms should now have set me free;
And I must wear the willow garland
  For him that's dead or false to me.'

'Nay! say not that his faith is tainted!'
  He raised his vizor — at the sight
She fell into his arms and fainted;
  It was indeed her own true knight!

T. Campbell

CVII

THE COUNCIL OF HORSES

UPON a time a neighing steed,
  Who graz'd among a numerous breed,
With mutiny had fired the train,
And spread dissension through the plain.
On matters that concern'd the state,
The council met in grand debate.
A colt whose eyeballs flamed with ire,
Elate with strength and youthful fire,
In haste stept forth before the rest,
And thus the listening throng address'd.

  'Goodness, how abject is our race,
Condemn'd to slavery and disgrace!
Shall we our servitude retain,
Because our sires have borne the chain?
Consider, friends! your strength and might;
'T is conquest to assert your right.
How cumbrous is the gilded coach!
The pride of man is our reproach.

Were we design'd for daily toil,
To drag the ploughshare through the soil,
To sweat in harness through the road,
To groan beneath the carrier's load?
How feeble are the two-legg'd kind!
What force is in our nerves combin'd!
Shall then our nobler jaws submit
To foam and champ the galling bit?
Shall haughty man my back bestride?
Shall the sharp spur provoke my side?
Forbid it, heavens! reject the rein;
Your shame, your infamy, disdain.
Let him the lion first control,
And still the tiger's famish'd growl.
Let us, like them, our freedom claim,
And make him tremble at our name.'

A general nod approv'd the cause,
And all the circle neigh'd applause.
When, lo! with grave and solemn pace,
A steed advanc'd before the race,
With age and long experience wise;
Around he cast his thoughtful eyes,
And, to the murmurs of the train,
Thus spoke the Nestor of the plain.

'When I had health and strength like you
The toils of servitude I knew;
Now grateful man rewards my pains,
And gives me all these wide domains.
At will I crop the year's increase;
My latter life is rest and peace.
I grant, to man we lend our pains,
And aid him to correct the plains;
But doth not he divide the care,
Through all the labours of the year?

How many thousand structures rise,
To fence us from inclement skies !
For us he bears the sultry day,
And stores up all our winter's hay.
He sows, he reaps the harvest's gain ;
We share the toil and share the grain.
Since every creature was decreed
To aid each other's mutual need,
Appease your discontented mind,
And act the part by heaven assign'd.'
　　The tumult ceas'd, the colt submitted,
And, like his ancestors, was bitted.

J. Gay

CVIII

ST. ROMUALD

ONE day, it matters not to know
　　How many hundred years ago,
A Frenchman stopt at an inn door :
The Landlord came to welcome him and chat
　　　　Of this and that,
For he had seen the traveller there before.
　　　'Doth holy Romuald dwell
　　　　Still in his cell ? '
The Traveller ask'd, 'or is the old man dead ? '
　　'No ; he has left his loving flock, and we
　　So great a Christian never more shall see,'
The Landlord answer'd, and he shook his head.
　　　' Ah, sir, we knew his worth !
　If ever there did live a saint on earth !
　Why, sir, he always used to wear a shirt
For thirty days, all seasons, day and night.

Good man, he knew it was not right,
For Dust and Ashes to fall out with Dirt !
And then he only hung it out in the rain,
    And put it on again.

'There has been perilous work
With him and the Devil there in yonder cell ;
For Satan used to maul him like a Turk.
    There they would sometimes fight,
        All through a winter's night,
            From sunset until morn.
He with a cross, the Devil with his horn ;
The Devil spitting fire with might and main,
    Enough to make St. Michael half afraid :
    He splashing holy water till he made
        His red hide hiss again,
And the hot vapour fill'd the smoking cell.
    This was so common that his face became
    All black and yellow with the brimstone flame,
And then he smelt . . . O dear, how he did smell !

'Then, sir, to see how he would mortify
    The flesh ! If any one had dainty fare,
        Good man, he would come there,
And look at all the delicate things, and cry,
        'O belly, belly,
    You would be gormandizing now, I know ;
            But it shall not be so !
Home to your bread and water, home, I tell ye !'

'But,' quoth the Traveller, 'wherefore did he leave
    A flock that knew his saintly worth so well ?'
    'Why,' said the Landlord, 'Sir, it so befell
        He heard unluckily of our intent

To do him a great honour ; and you know
He was not covetous of fame below,
And so by stealth one night away he went.'

'What might this honour be?' the Traveller cried.
    'Why, sir,' the host replied,
'We thought perhaps that he might one day leave us ;
    And then should strangers have
        The good man's grave.
A loss like that would naturally grieve us,
    For he'll be made a saint of, to be sure.
    Therefore we thought it prudent to secure
        His relics while we might ;
And so we meant to strangle him one night.'

                                    R. Southey

CIX

LADY ALICE

LADY ALICE was sitting in her bower window
    At midnight mending her quoif ;
And there she saw as fine a corpse
    As ever she saw in her life.

'What bear ye, what bear ye, ye six men tall?
    What bear ye on your shoulders?'
'We bear the corpse of Giles Collins,
    An old and true lover of yours.'

'Oh, lay him down gently, ye six men tall,
    All on the grass so green,
And to-morrow when the sun goes down,
    Lady Alice a corpse shall be seen.

15

'And bury me in Saint Mary's church,
　　All for my love so true ;
And make me a garland of marjoram,
　　And of lemon-thyme, and rue.'

Giles Collins was buried all in the east,
　　Lady Alice all in the west ;
And the roses that grew on Giles Collins's grave,
　　They reached Lady Alice's breast.

The priest of the parish he chanced to pass,
　　And he severed those roses in twain.
Sure never were seen such true lovers before,
　　Nor e'er will there be again.
　　　　　　　　　　　　　　　Old Ballad

CX

THE OUTLANDISH KNIGHT

AN outlandish knight came from the North lands,
　　And he came a wooing to me ;
And he told me he'd take me unto the North lands,
　　And there he would marry me.

'Come, fetch me some of your father's gold,
　　And some of your mother's fee ;
And two of the best nags out of the stable,
　　Where they stand thirty and three.'

She fetched him some of her father's gold
　　And some of her mother's fee ;
And two of the best nags out of the stable,
　　Where they stood thirty and three.

She mounted her on her milk-white steed,
   He on the dapple-gray ;
They rode till they came unto the sea-side,
   Three hours before it was day.

' Light off, light off thy milk-white steed,
   And deliver it unto me ;
Six pretty maids have I drowned here,
   And thou the seventh shall be.

' Pull off, pull off thy silken gown,
   And deliver it unto me,
Methinks it looks too rich and too gay
   To rot in the salt sea.

' Pull off, pull off thy silken stays,
   And deliver them unto me !
Methinks they are too fine and gay
   To rot in the salt sea.

' Pull off, pull off thy Holland smock,
   And deliver it unto me ;
Methinks it looks too rich and gay
   To rot in the salt sea.'

' If I must pull off my Holland smock,
   Pray turn thy back unto me,
For it is not fitting that such a ruffian
   A woman unclad should see.'

He turned his back towards her,
   And viewed the leaves so green ;
She catch'd him round the middle so small,
   And tumbled him into the stream.

He dropped high, and he dropped low,
　　Until he came to the tide, —
'Catch hold of my hand, my pretty maiden,
　　And I will make you my bride.'

'Lie there, lie there, you false-hearted man,
　　Lie there instead of me ;
Six pretty maidens have you drowned here,
　　And the seventh has drowned thee.'

She mounted on her milk-white steed,
　　And led the dapple gray.
She rode till she came to her father's hall,
　　Three hours before it was day.

Old Ballad

CXI

SPRING

SPRING, the sweet Spring, is the year's pleasant
　　king ;
Then blooms each thing, then maids dance in a ring ;
Cold doth not sting, the pretty birds do sing,
Cuckoo, jug-jug, pu-we, to-witta-woo !

The palm and the may make country houses gay,
Lambs frisk and play, the shepherds pipe all day,
And we hear aye birds tune this merry lay,
Cuckoo, jug-jug, pu-we, to-witta-woo !

The fields breathe sweet, the daisies kiss our feet,
Young lovers meet, old wives a sunning sit,

In every street these tunes our ears do greet,
Cuckoo, jug-jug, pu-we, to-witta-woo.
    Spring, the sweet Spring.
             T. Nash

CXII

SWEET WILLIAM'S GHOST

THERE came a ghost to Margaret's door,
    With many a grievous groan,
And aye he tirled at the pin,
    But answer made she none.

'Is that my father Philip,
    Or is 't my brother John?
Or is 't my true love Willy,
    From Scotland new come home?'

''T is not thy father Philip,
    Nor yet thy brother John;
But 't is thy true love Willy,
    From Scotland new come home.

'O sweet Margaret, O dear Margaret,
    I pray thee speak to me:
Give me my faith and troth, Margaret,
    As I gave it to thee.'

'Thy faith and troth thou 'lt never get,
    Nor yet wilt thou me win,
Till that thou come within my bower
    And kiss my cheek and chin.'

'If I should come within thy bower,
　　I am no earthly man :
And should I kiss thy rosy lips
　　Thy days would not be lang.

'O sweet Margaret, O dear Margaret,
　　I pray thee speak to me :
Give me my faith and troth, Margaret,
　　As I gave it to thee.'

'Thy faith and troth thou 'lt never get,
　　Nor yet wilt thou me win,
Till you take me to yon kirk-yard,
　　And wed me with a ring.'

'My bones are buried in yon kirk-yard
　　Afar beyond the sea,
And it is but my spirit, Margaret,
　　That's now speaking to thee.'

She stretched out her lily-white hand,
　　And for to do her best :
'Have there your faith and troth, Willy,
　　God send your soul good rest.'

Now she has kilted her robes of green
　　A piece below her knee ;
And all the live-long winter night
　　The dead corpse followed she.

'Is there any room at your head, Willy,
　　Or any room at your feet ;
Or any room at your side, Willy,
　　Wherein that I may creep ?'

'There's no room at my head, Margaret,
  There's no room at my feet;
There's no room at my side, Margaret,
  My coffin's made so meet;

Then up and crew the red red cock,
  And up then crew the gray;
''T is time, 't is time, my dear Margaret,
  That you were going away.'

Old Ballad

CXIII

THE FOUNTAIN

INTO the sunshine,
    Full of the light,
  Leaping and flashing
    From morn till night!

  Into the moonlight,
    Whiter than snow,
  Waving so flower-like
    When the winds blow!

  Into the starlight,
    Rushing in spray,
  Happy at midnight,
    Happy by day!

  Ever in motion,
    Blithesome and cheery,
  Still climbing heavenward,
    Never aweary;

Glad of all weathers,
  Still seeming best,
Upward or downward
  Motion thy rest;

Full of a nature
  Nothing can tame,
Changed every moment,
  Ever the same;

Ceaseless aspiring,
  Ceaseless content,
Darkness or sunshine
  Thy element;

Glorious fountain!
  Let my heart be
Fresh, changeful, constant,
  Upward like thee!

                    J. R. Lowell

CXIV

FAIR ROSAMUND

WHEN as King Henry ruled this land
    The second of that name,
Above all else, he dearly loved
  A fair and comely dame.

Her crisped locks like threads of gold
  Appear'd to each man's sight;
Her sparkling eyes, like orient pearls,
  Did cast a heavenly light.

The blood within her crystal cheeks
   Did such a colour drive,
As though the lily and the rose
   For mastership did strive.

Yea Rosamund, fair Rosamund,
   Her name was called so,
To whom our queen, queen Ellinor
   Was known a deadly foe.

The king therefore, for her defence
   Against the furious queen,
At Woodstock builded such a bower,
   The like was never seen.

Most curiously that bower was built,
   Of stone and timber strong ;
An hundred and fifty doors
   Did to this bower belong,

And they so cunningly contrived,
   With turnings round about,
That none, but with a clue of thread,
   Could enter in and out.

And for his love and lady's sake,
   That was so fair and bright,
The keeping of this bower he gave
   Unto a valiant knight.

But fortune, that doth often frown
   Where she before did smile,
The king's delight and lady's joy
   Full soon she did beguile :

For why ? the king's ungracious son,
   Whom he did high advance,
Against his father raised wars,
   Within the realm of France.

But yet before our comely king
   The English land forsook,
Of Rosamund, his lady fair,
   His farewell thus he took :

'My Rosamund, my only rose,
   That pleaseth best mine eye :
The fairest flower in all the world
   To feed my fantasy ;

'The flower of mine affected heart,
   Whose sweetness doth excel
All roses else a thousand times,
   I bid thee now farewell.'

When Rosamund, that lady bright,
   Did hear the king say so,
The sorrow of her grieved heart
   Her outward looks did show ;

And from her clear and crystal eyes
   The tears gush'd out apace,
Which like the silver pearled dew
   Ran down her comely face.

'Why grieves my Rose, my sweetest Rose ?'
   The king did often say.
'Because,' quoth she, ' to bloody wars
   My lord must part away.

'But since your Grace on foreign coasts,
  Among your foes unkind,
Must go to hazard life and limb,
  Why should I stay behind?

'Nay, rather let me, like a page,
  Your sword and target bear,
That on my breast the blows may light,
  Which would offend you there.

'So I your presence may enjoy,
  No toil I will refuse;
But wanting you, my life is death;
  Nay, death I'd rather choose!'

'Content thyself, my dearest love,
  Thy rest at home shall be
In England's sweet and pleasant isle;
  For travel fits not thee.

'My Rose shall safely here abide,
  With music pass the day;
Whilst I, among the piercing pikes,
  My foes seek far away.

'And you, Sir Thomas, whom I trust
  To be my love's defence;
Be careful of my gallant Rose
  When I am parted hence.'

And therewithal he fetch'd a sigh
  As though his heart would break:
And Rosamund, for very grief,
  Not one plain word could speak.

And at their parting well they might
  In heart be grieved sore :
After that day fair Rosamund
  The king did see no more.

For when his Grace had past the seas,
  And into France was gone,
With envious heart queen Ellinor
  To Woodstock came anone.

And forth she calls this trusty knight
  In an unhappy hour ;
Who with his clue of twined thread
  Came from this famous bower.

And when that they had wounded him
  The queen this thread did get,
And went, where lady Rosamund
  Was like an angel set.

But when the queen with steadfast eye
  Beheld her beauteous face,
She was amazed in her mind
  At her exceeding grace.

'Cast off from thee those robes,' she said,
  'That rich and costly be ;
And drink thou up this deadly draught,
  Which I have brought to thee.'

Then presently upon her knees
  Sweet Rosamund did fall ;
And pardon of the queen she craved
  For her offences all.

' Take pity on my youthful years,'
   Fair Rosamund did cry ;
' And let me not with poison strong
   Enforced be to die.'

And with these words, her lily hands
   She wrung full often there ;
And down along her lovely face
   Did trickle many a tear.

But nothing could this furious queen
   Therewith appeased be ;
The cup of deadly poison strong,
   As she knelt on her knee,

She gave this comely dame to drink,
   Who took it in her hand,
And from her bended knee arose,
   And on her feet did stand ;

And casting up her eyes to heaven
   She did for mercy call ;
And drinking up the poison strong,
   Her life she lost withal.

And when that death through every limb
   Had showed its greatest spite,
Her chiefest foes did plain confess
   She was a glorious wight.

Her body then they did entomb,
   When life was fled away,
At Godstowe, near to Oxford town,
   As may be seen this day.

               T. Delone

CXV

THE HITCHEN MAY–DAY SONG

REMEMBER us poor Mayers all !
   And thus we do begin
To lead our lives in righteousness,
   Or else we die in sin.

We have been rambling all the night,
   And almost all the day ;
And now returned back again,
   We have brought you a branch of **May**.

A branch of May we have brought you,
   And at your door it stands ;
It is but a sprout, but it 's well budded out
   By the work of our Lord's hands.

The hedges and trees they are so **green**,
   As green as any leek ;
Our heavenly Father He water'd them
   With His heavenly dew so sweet.

The heavenly gates are open wide,
   Our paths are beaten plain ;
And if a man be not too far gone,
   He may return again.

The life of man is but a span,
   It flourishes like a flower ;
We are here to-day and gone to-morrow,
   And we are dead in an hour.

The moon shines bright, and the stars give a light,
  A little before it is day :
So God bless you all, both great and small,
  And send you a joyful May !

Old Song

CXVI

THE SPANISH LADY'S LOVE

WILL you hear a Spanish lady
    How she woo'd an English man ?
Garments gay and rich as may be,
  Decked with jewels, had she on ;
Of a comely countenance and grace was she,
And by birth and parentage of high degree.

As his prisoner there he kept her,
  In his hands her life did lie ;
Cupid's bands did tie her faster,
  By the liking of an eye ;
In his courteous company was all her joy,
To favour him in any thing she was not coy.

At the last there came commandment
  For to set the ladies free,
With their jewels still adorned,
  None to do them injury :
' Alas ! ' then said this lady gay, ' full woe is me ;
O let me still sustain this kind captivity !

' O gallant captain, show some pity
  To a lady in distress ;

Leave me not within the city,
    For to die in heaviness ;
Thou hast set this present day my body free,
But my heart in prison strong remains with thee.'

' How shouldst thou, fair lady, love me,
    Whom thou know'st thy country's foe ?
Thy fair words make me suspect thee ;
    Serpents are where flowers grow.'
' All the evil I think to thee, most gracious knight,
God grant unto myself the same may fully light :

' Blessed be the time and season
    That you came on Spanish ground ;
If you may our foes be termed,
    Gentle foes we have you found.
With our city you have won our hearts each one ;
Then to your country bear away that is your own.'

' Rest you still, most gallant lady,
    Rest you still, and weep no more ;
Of fair lovers there are plenty ;
    Spain doth yield a wondrous store.'
' Spaniards fraught with jealousy we often find,
But English men throughout the world are counted
            kind.

' Leave me not unto a Spaniard ;
    You alone enjoy my heart ;
I am lovely, young, and tender,
    And so love is my desert.
Still to serve thee day and night my mind is press'd ;
The wife of every English man is counted blest.'

'It would be a shame, fair lady,
   For to bear a woman hence ;
English soldiers never carry
   Any such without offence.'
'I will quickly change myself if it be so,
And like a page I 'll follow thee where'er thou go.'

'I have neither gold nor silver
   To maintain thee in this case,
And to travel, 't is great charges,
   As you know, in every place.'
'My chains and jewels every one shall be thine own,
And eke five hundred pounds in gold that lies unknown.'

'On the seas are many dangers ;
   Many storms do there arise,
Which will be to ladies dreadful,
   And force tears from watery eyes.'
'Well in truth I shall endure extremity,
For I could find in heart to lose my life for thee.'

'Courteous lady, be contented ;
   Here comes all that breeds the strife ;
I in England have already
   A sweet woman to my wife :
I will not falsify my vow for gold or gain,
Nor yet for all the fairest dames that live in Spain.'

'Oh how happy is that woman,
   That enjoys so true a friend !
Many days of joy God send you !
   Of my suit I 'll make an end :
On my knees I pardon crave for this offence,
Which did from love and true affection first commence.

16

'Commend me to thy loving lady :
　Bear to her this chain of gold,
And these bracelets for a token ;
　Grieving that I was so bold.
All my jewels in like sort bear thou with thee,
For they are fitting for thy wife, but not for me.

'I will spend my days in prayer,
　Love and all her laws defy,
In a nunnery will I shroud me,
　Far from any company :
But ere my prayers have an end, be sure of this,
To pray for thee and for thy love I will not miss.

'Thus farewell, most gentle captain,
　And farewell my heart 's content !
Count not Spanish ladies wayward,
　Though to thee my love was bent :
Joy and true prosperity go still with thee !'
'The like fall ever to thy share, most fair lady.'

　　　　　　　　　　　　　　Old Ballad

CXVII

LITTLE WHITE LILY

LITTLE white Lily
 Sat by a stone,
Drooping and waiting
Till the sun shone.
Little white Lily
Sunshine has fed ;
Little white Lily
Is lifting her head.

Little white Lily
Said, ' It is good ;
Little white Lily's
Clothing and food.'
Little white Lily,
Drest like a bride !
Shining with whiteness,
And crown'd beside !

Little white Lily
Droopeth with pain,
Waiting and waiting
For the wet rain.
Little white Lily
Holdeth her cup ;
Rain is fast falling
And filling it up.

Little white Lily
Said, ' Good again,

When I am thirsty
To have nice rain ;
Now I am stronger,
Now I am cool ;
Heat cannot burn me,
My veins are so full.'

Little white Lily
Smells very sweet :
On her head sunshine,
Rain at her feet.
' Thanks to the sunshine,
Thanks to the rain !
Little white Lily
Is happy again !'

G. MacDonald

CXVIII

MINSTREL'S SONG IN ELLA

O SING unto my roundelay ;
    O drop the briny tear with me ;
Dance no more at holiday ;
    Like a running river be ;
        My love is dead,
        Gone to his death-bed,
        All under the willow-tree.

Black his hair as the winter night,
    White his neck as summer snow,
Ruddy his face as the morning light,
    Cold he lies in the grave below.

My love is dead,
Gone to his death-bed,
All under the willow-tree.

Sweet his tongue as throstle's note,
   Quick in dance as thought can be ;
Deft his tabor, cudgel stout ;
   O, he lies by the willow-tree !
      My love is dead,
      Gone to his death-bed,
      All under the willow-tree.

Hark ! the raven flaps his wing
   In the brier'd dell below ;
Hark ! the death-owl loud doth sing
   To the night-mares as they go.
      My love is dead,
      Gone to his death-bed,
      All under the willow-tree.

See, the white moon shines on high ;
   Whiter is my true love's shroud ;
Whiter than the morning sky,
   Whiter than the evening cloud.
      My love is dead,
      Gone to his death-bed,
      All under the willow-tree.

                  T. Chatterton

CXIX

AN ELEGY ON THE DEATH OF A MAD DOG

GOOD people all, of every sort,
   Give ear unto my song ;
And if you find it wondrous short,
   It cannot hold you long.

In Islington there was a man,
   Of whom the world might say,
That still a godly race he ran
   Whene'er he went to pray.

A kind and gentle heart he had,
   To comfort friends and foes ;
The naked every day he clad,
   When he put on his clothes.

And in that town a dog was found,
   As many dogs there be,
Both mongrel, puppy, whelp, and hound,
   And curs of low degree.

This dog and man at first were friends ;
   But when a pique began,
The dog, to gain his private ends,
   Went mad, and bit the man.

Around from all the neighbouring streets
   The wondering neighbours ran,
And swore the dog had lost his wits,
   To bite so good a man.

The wound it seem'd both sore and sad
　　To every Christian eye :
And while they swore the dog was mad,
　　They swore the man would die.

But soon a wonder came to light,
　　That show'd the rogues they lied,
The man recover'd of the bite,
　　The dog it was that died.

　　　　　　　　　　O. Goldsmith

CXX

NONGTONGPAW

JOHN Bull for pastime took a prance,
　　Some time ago, to peep at France ;
To talk of sciences and arts,
And knowledge gain'd in foreign parts.
Monsieur, obsequious, heard him speak,
And answer'd John in heathen Greek :
To all he ask'd, 'bout all he saw,
'T was, ' Monsieur, je vous n'entends pas.'

John, to the Palais Royal come,
Its splendour almost struck him dumb.
' I say, whose house is that there here ? '
' House !　Je vous n'entends pas, Monsieur.'
' What, Nongtongpaw again ! ' cries John ;
' This fellow is some mighty Don :
No doubt he 's plenty for the maw,
I 'll breakfast with this Nongtongpaw.'

John saw Versailles from Marli's height,
And cried, astonish'd at the sight,
' Whose fine estate is that there here?'
' State !   Je vous n'entends pas, Monsieur.'
' His? what, the land and houses too ?
The fellow 's richer than a Jew :
On everything he lays his claw !
I should like to dine with Nongtongpaw.'

Next tripping came a courtly fair,
John cried, enchanted with her air,
' What lovely wench is that there here?'
' Ventch !   Je vous n'entends pas, Monsieur.'
' What, he again ?   Upon my life !
A palace, lands, and then a wife
Sir Joshua might delight to draw :
I should like to sup with Nongtongpaw.

' But hold ! whose funeral 's that?' cries John.
' Je vous n'entends pas.' — ' What, is he gone?
Wealth, fame, and beauty could not save
Poor Nongtongpaw then from the grave !
His race is run, his game is up, —
I 'd with him breakfast, dine, and sup ;
But since he chooses to withdraw,
Good night t' ye, Mounseer Nongtongpaw !'

C. Dibdin

CXXI

POOR DOG TRAY

ON the green banks of Shannon when Sheelah was
nigh,
No blithe Irish lad was so happy as I ;
No harp like my own could so cheerily play,
And wherever I went was my poor dog Tray.

When at last I was forced from my Sheelah to part,
She said, (while the sorrow was big at her heart,)
Oh ! remember your Sheelah when far, far away :
And be kind, my dear Pat, to our poor dog Tray.

Poor dog ! he was faithful and kind to be sure,
And he constantly loved me although I was poor ;
When the sour-looking folk sent me heartless away,
I had always a friend in my poor dog Tray.

When the road was so dark, and the night was so cold,
And Pat and his dog were grown weary and old,
How snugly we slept in my old coat of gray,
And he lick'd me for kindness — my old dog Tray.

Though my wallet was scant I remember'd his case,
Nor refused my last crust to his pitiful face ;
But he died at my feet on a cold winter day,
And I play'd a sad lament for my poor dog Tray.

Where now shall I go, poor, forsaken, and blind ?
Can I find one to guide me, so faithful and kind ?
To my sweet native village, so far, far away,
I can never more return with my poor dog Tray.
T. Campbell

CXXII

THE FAITHFUL BIRD

THE greenhouse is my summer seat ;
　My shrubs, displaced from that retreat,
　　Enjoy'd the open air ;
Two goldfinches, whose sprightly song
Had been their mutual solace long,
　　Lived happy prisoners there.

They sang as blithe as finches sing
That flutter loose on golden wing,
　　And frolic where they list ;
Strangers to liberty, 't is true,
But that delight they never knew,
　　And therefore never miss'd.

But nature works in every breast,
With force not easily suppress'd ;
　　And Dick felt some desires,
That, after many an effort vain,
Instructed him at length to gain
　　A pass between the wires.

The open windows seem'd to invite
The freeman to a farewell flight ;
　　But Tom was still confin'd ;
And Dick, although his way was clear,
Was much too generous and sincere
　　To leave his friend behind.

So, settling on his cage, by play,
And chirp, and kiss, he seem'd to say,
　　You must not live alone —

Nor would he quit that chosen stand,
Till I, with slow and cautious hand,
　　Return'd him to his own.
　　　　　　　　W. Cowper

CXXIII

LORD ULLIN'S DAUGHTER

A CHIEFTAIN to the Highlands bound
　　Cries, 'Boatman, do not tarry!
And I'll give thee a silver pound
　　To row us o'er the ferry.'

'Now who be ye, would cross Lochgyle,
　　This dark and stormy water?'
'O, I'm the chief of Ulva's isle,
　　And this Lord Ullin's daughter.

'And fast before her father's men
　　Three days we've fled together,
For should he find us in the glen,
　　My blood would stain the heather.

'His horsemen hard behind us ride;
　　Should they our steps discover,
Then who will cheer my bonny bride
　　When they have slain her lover?'

Out spoke the hardy Highland wight,
　　'I'll go, my chief, I'm ready;
It is not for your silver bright;
　　But for your winsome lady:.

'And by my word ! the bonny bird
  In danger shall not tarry :
So though the waves are raging white,
  I 'll row you o'er the ferry.'

By this the storm grew loud apace,
  The water-wraith was shrieking ;
And in the scowl of Heaven each face
  Grew dark as they were speaking.

But still as wilder blew the wind,
  And as the night grew drearer,
Adown the glen rode armed men,
  Their trampling sounded nearer.

'O haste thee, haste !' the lady cries,
  'Though tempests round us gather ;
I 'll meet the raging of the skies,
  But not an angry father.'

The boat has left the stormy land,
  A stormy sea before her, —
When, oh ! too strong for human hand
  The tempest gathered o'er her.

And still they row'd amidst the roar
  Of waters fast prevailing :
Lord Ullin reach'd that fatal shore ;
  His wrath was changed to wailing.

For, sore dismay'd, through storm and shade
  His child he did discover :
One lovely hand she stretch'd for aid,
  And one was round her lover.

'Come back ! come back !' he cried in grief,
　　'Across this stormy water :
And I 'll forgive your Highland chief,
　　My daughter ! oh, my daughter !'

'T was vain : the loud waves lash'd the shore,
　　Return or aid preventing ;
The waters wild went o'er his child,
　　And he was left lamenting.
T. Campbell

CXXIV

THE SEA

TO sea ! to sea ! the calm is o'er,
　　The wanton water leaps in sport,
And rattles down the pebbly shore,
　　The dolphin wheels, the sea-cows snort,
And unseen mermaid's pearly song
Comes bubbling up, the weeds among.
Fling broad the sail, dip deep the oar :
To sea ! to sea ! the calm is o'er.

To sea ! to sea ! our white winged bark
　　Shall billowing cleave its watery way,
And with its shadow, fleet and dark,
　　Break the caved Tritons' azure day,
Like mountain eagle soaring light
O'er antelopes on Alpine height.
The anchor heaves ! The ship swings free !
Our sails swell full ! To sea ! to sea !
T. L. Beddoes

CXXV

FIDELITY

A BARKING sound the shepherd hears,
A cry as of a dog or fox ;
He halts, and searches with his eye
Among the scattered rocks :
And now at distance can discern
A stirring in a brake of fern ;
And instantly a dog is seen,
Glancing through that covert green.

The dog is not of mountain breed ;
Its motions, too, are wild and shy ;
With something, as the shepherd thinks,
Unusual in its cry :
Nor is there any one in sight
All round, in hollow or on height ;
Nor shout, nor whistle strikes his ear :
What is the creature doing here ?

It was a cove, a huge recess,
That keeps, till June, December's snow ;
A lofty precipice in front,
A silent tarn below ;
Far in the bosom of Helvellyn,
Remote from public road or dwelling,
Pathway, or cultivated land ;
From trace of human foot or hand.

.There sometimes doth a leaping fish
.Send through the tarn a lonely cheer ;

The crags repeat the raven's croak,
In symphony austere ;
Thither the rainbow comes, the cloud —
And mists that spread the flying shroud,
And sunbeams ; and the sounding blast,
That if it could would hurry past ;
But that enormous barrier holds it fast.

Not free from boding thoughts, awhile
The shepherd stood, then makes his way
O'er rocks and stones, following the dog
As quickly as he may ;
Nor far had gone before he found
A human skeleton on the ground :
The appalled discoverer with a sigh
Looks round to learn the history.

From those abrupt and perilous rocks
The man had fallen, that place of fear !
At length upon the shepherd's mind
It breaks, and all is clear :
He instantly recalled the name,
And who he was, and whence he came ;
Remembered too the very day
On which the traveller passed that way.

But here a wonder for whose sake
This lamentable tale I tell !
A lasting monument of words
This wonder merits well.
The dog, which still was hovering nigh,
Repeating the same timid cry,
This dog had been through three months' space
A dweller in that savage place.

Yes, proof was plain that since the day
When this ill-fated traveller died,
The dog had watch'd about the spot,
Or by his master's side :
How nourished there through that long time,
He knows who gave that love sublime ;
And gave that strength of feeling great,
Above all human estimate.

W. Wordsworth

CXXVI

THE FOX AND THE CAT

THE fox and the cat, as they travell'd one day,
 With moral discourses cut shorter the way :
' 'T is great,' says the Fox, ' to make justice our guide ! '
' How god-like is mercy ! ' Grimalkin replied.
 Whilst thus they proceeded, a wolf from the wood,
Impatient of hunger, and thirsting for blood,
Rush'd forth — as he saw the dull shepherd asleep —
And seiz'd for his supper an innocent sheep.
' In vain, wretched victim, for mercy you bleat,
When mutton 's at hand,' says the wolf, ' I must eat.'
 Grimalkin 's astonish'd ! — the fox stood aghast,
To see the fell beast at his bloody repast.
' What a wretch,' says the cat, ' 't is the vilest of brutes ;
Does he feed upon flesh when there 's herbage and
  roots ? '
Cries the fox, ' While our oaks give us acorns so good,
What a tyrant is this to spill innocent blood ! '
 Well, onward they march'd, and they moraliz'd still,
Till they came where some poultry pick'd chaff by a
  mill.

Sly Reynard survey'd them with gluttonous eyes,
And made, spite of morals, a pullet his prize.
A mouse, too, that chanc'd from her covert to stray,
The greedy Grimalkin secured as her prey.

  A spider, that sat in her web on the wall,
Perceiv'd the poor victims, and pitied their fall ;
She cried, ' Of such murders, how guiltless am I ! '
So ran to regale on a new-taken fly.

J. Cunningham

CXXVII

THE DOG AND THE WATER-LILY

THE noon was shady, and soft airs
   Swept Ouse's silent tide,
When, 'scaped from literary cares,
   I wander'd on his side.

My spaniel, prettiest of his race,
   And high in pedigree, —
(Two nymphs adorn'd with every grace
   That spaniel found for me,) —

Now wanton'd lost in flags and reeds,
   Now, starting into sight,
Pursued the swallow o'er the meads
   With scarce a slower flight.

It was the time when Ouse display'd
   His lilies newly blown ;
Their beauties I intent survey'd,
   And one I wish'd my own.

With cane extended far I sought
　　To steer it close to land ;
But still the prize, though nearly caught,
　　Escaped my eager hand.

Beau mark'd my unsuccessful pains
　　With fix'd considerate face,
And puzzling set his puppy brains
　　To comprehend the case.

But, with a chirrup clear and strong,
　　Dispersing all his dream,
I thence withdrew, and follow'd long
　　The windings of the stream.

My ramble ended, I return'd ;
　　Beau trotted far before,
The floating wreath again discern'd,
　　And plunging, left the shore.

I saw him with that lily cropp'd,
　　Impatient swim to meet
My quick approach, and soon he dropp'd
　　The treasure at my feet.

Charm'd with the sight, ' The world,' I cried,
　　' Shall hear of this thy deed ;
My dog shall mortify the pride
　　Of man's superior breed ;

' But chief myself I will enjoin,
　　Awake at duty's call,
To show a love as prompt as thine
　　To Him who gives me all.'

　　　　　　　　　　　　　W. Cowper

CXXVIII

AN EPITAPH ON A ROBIN-REDBREAST

TREAD lightly here, for here, 't is said,
  When piping winds are hush'd around,
A small note wakes from underground,
Where now his tiny bones are laid.
No more in lone or leafless groves,
With ruffled wing and faded breast,
His friendless, homeless spirit roves ;
Gone to the world where birds are blest !
Where never cat glides o'er the green,
Or school-boy's giant form is seen ;
But love, and joy, and smiling Spring
Inspire their little souls to sing !

                                        S. Rogers

CXXIX

BAUCIS AND PHILEMON

IN ancient times, as story tells,
  The saints would often leave their cells,
And stroll about, but hide their quality,
To try good people's hospitality.
  It happen'd on a winter night,
As authors of the legend write,
Two brother hermits, saints by trade,
Taking their tour in masquerade,
Disguis'd in tatter'd habits went
To a small village down in Kent ;
Where, in the stroller's canting strain,
They begg'd from door to door in vain,

Tried every tone might pity win ;
But not a soul would take them in.
   Our wandering saints, in woful state,
Treated at this ungodly rate,
Having through all the village past,
To a small cottage came at last
Where dwelt a good old honest yeoman
Call'd in the neighbourhood Philemon ;
Who kindly did these saints invite
In his poor hut to pass the night ;
And then the hospitable sire
Bid goody Baucis mend the fire ;
While he from out the chimney took
A flitch of bacon off the hook,
And freely from the fattest side
Cut out large slices to be fried ;
Then stepp'd aside to fetch them drink,
Fill'd a large jug up to the brink,
And saw it fairly twice go round ;
Yet (what is wonderful !) they found
'T was still replenish'd to the top,
As if they ne'er had touch'd a drop.
The good old couple were amaz'd,
And often on each other gaz'd ;
For both were frightened to the heart,
And just began to cry, ' What ar't ! '
Then softly turn'd aside to view
Whether the lights were burning blue.
' Good folks, you need not be afraid,
We are but saints,' the hermits said ;
' No hurt shall come to you or yours :
But for that pack of churlish boors,
Not fit to live on Christian ground,
They and their houses shall be drown'd ;

Whilst you shall see your cottage rise,
And grow a church before your eyes.'
    They scarce had spoke when fair and soft
The roof began to mount aloft,
Aloft rose every beam and rafter,
The heavy wall climb'd slowly after;
The chimney widen'd and grew higher,
Became a steeple with a spire.
    The kettle to the top was hoist,
And there stood fasten'd to a joist;
Doom'd ever in suspense to dwell,
'T is now no kettle, but a bell.
    A wooden jack which had almost
Lost by disuse the art to roast,
A sudden alteration feels,
Increas'd by new intestine wheels;
The jack and chimney, near allied,
Had never left each other's side:
The chimney to a steeple grown,
The jack would not be left alone;
But up against the steeple rear'd,
Became a clock, and still adhered.
    The groaning chair began to crawl,
Like a huge snail, along the wall;
There stuck aloft in public view,
And with small change a pulpit grew.
    The cottage, by such feats as these,
Grown to a church by just degrees,
The hermits then desired the host
To ask for what he fancied most.
Philemon, having paus'd awhile,
Return'd them thanks in homely style:
' I 'm old, and fain would live at ease;
Make me the parson, if you please.'

Thus happy in their change of life
Were several years this man and wife.
When on a day, which prov'd their last,
Discoursing on old stories past,
They went by chance, amidst their talk,
To the churchyard to take a walk ;
When Baucis hastily cried out,
'My dear, I see your forehead sprout !'
'Sprout !' quoth the man ; 'what's this you tell us ?
I hope you don't believe me jealous !
But yet, methinks, I feel it true ;
And really yours is budding too —
Nay, — now I cannot stir my foot ;
It feels as if 't were taking root.'
Description would but tire my muse ;
In short, they both were turn'd to yews.

J. Swift

CXXX

LULLABY FOR TITANIA

First Fairy

YOU spotted snakes with double tongue,
   Thorny hedgehogs, be not seen ;
Newts, and blind-worms, do no wrong ;
   Come not near our fairy queen.

Chorus

Philomel with melody
Sing in our sweet lullaby !
Lulla, lulla, lullaby ; lulla, lulla, lullaby !

Never harm, nor spell, nor charm,
    Come our lovely lady nigh !
    So good-night, with lullaby.

Second Fairy

Weaving spiders, come not here ;
    Hence, you long-legg'd spinners, hence ;
Beetles black, approach not near ;
    Worm, nor snail, do no offence.

Chorus

    Philomel with melody
    Sing in our sweet lullaby ;
Lulla, lulla, lullaby ; lulla, lulla, lullaby !
Never harm, nor spell, nor charm,
    Come our lovely lady nigh !
    So good-night, with lullaby.
                W. Shakespeare

CXXXI

LORD THOMAS AND FAIR ELLINOR

LORD Thomas he was a bold forester,
    And a chaser of the king's deer ;
Fair Ellinor was a fine woman,
    And Lord Thomas he loved her dear.

'Come riddle my riddle, dear mother,' he said,
    'And riddle us both as one ;
Whether I shall marry with fair Ellinor,
    And let the brown girl alone ? '

'The brown girl she has got houses and land,
   And fair Ellinor she has got none ;
Therefore I charge you on my blessing,
   Bring me the brown girl home.'

As it befell on a high holiday,
   As many more did beside,
Lord Thomas he went to fair Ellinor,
   That should have been his bride.

But when he came to fair Ellinor's bower,
   He knocked there at the ring ;
But who was so ready as fair Ellinor
   For to let Lord Thomas in.

' What news, what news, Lord Thomas ? ' she said,
   ' What news hast thou brought unto me ? '
' I am come to bid thee to my wedding,
   And that is bad news for thee.'

' O, God forbid, Lord Thomas,' she said,
   ' That such a thing should be done.
I thought to have been thy bride my own self,
   And you to have been the bridegroom.'

' Come riddle my riddle, dear mother,' she said,
   ' And riddle it all in one ;
Whether I shall go to Lord Thomas's wedding,
   Or whether I shall tarry at home ? '

' There are many that are your friends, daughter,
   And many that are your foe ;
Therefore I charge you on my blessing,
   To Lord Thomas's wedding don't go.'

' There 's many that are my friends, mother,
    And if a thousand more were my foe,
Betide my life, betide my death,
    To Lord Thomas's wedding I 'll go.'

She clothed herself in gallant attire,
    And her merry men all in green ;
And as they rid through every town,
    They took her to be some queen.

But when she came to Lord Thomas's gate,
    She knocked there at the ring ;
But who was so ready as Lord Thomas
    To let fair Ellinor in.

' Is this your bride ? ' fair Ellinor said ;
    ' Methinks she looks wonderful brown ;
Thou might'st have had as fair a woman,
    As ever trod on the ground.'

' Despise her not, fair Ellin,' he said,
    ' Despise her not unto me ;
For better I love thy little finger,
    Than all her whole body.'

This brown bride had a little penknife,
    That was both long and sharp,
And betwixt the short ribs and the long,
    Prick'd fair Ellinor to the heart.

' Now Heaven save thee,' Lord Thomas he said,
    ' Methinks thou look'st wondrous wan :
Thou used to look with as fresh a colour,
    As ever the sun shined on.'

' O, art thou blind, Lord Thomas?' she said,
  ' Or canst thou not very well see?
O, dost thou not see my own heart's blood
  Run trickling down my knee?'

Lord Thomas he had a sword by his side;
  As he walked about the hall,
He cut off his bride's head from her shoulders,
  And threw it against the wall.

He set the hilt against the ground,
  And the point against his heart;
There never were three lovers met,
  That sooner did depart.

Old Ballad

CXXXII

QUEEN MAB

O THEN, I see, Queen Mab hath been with you.
  She is the fairies' midwife, and she comes
In shape no bigger than an agate stone
On the forefinger of an alderman;
Drawn with a team of little atomies
Athwart men's noses as they lie asleep:
Her wagon spokes made of long spinner's legs:
The cover, of the wings of grasshoppers;
The traces, of the smallest spider's web;
The collars of the moonshine's watery beams;
Her whip of cricket's bone, the lash, of film;
Her wagoner, a small gray-coated gnat,
Not half so big as a round little worm,
Pricked from the lazy finger of a maid:

Her chariot is an empty hazel nut,
Made by the joiner squirrel, or old grub,
Time out of mind the fairies' coachmakers.
And in this state she gallops night by night,
Through lovers' brains, and then they dream of love ;
On courtiers' knees that dream on court'sies straight ;
O'er lawyers' fingers, who straight dream on fees ;
O'er ladies' lips, who straight on kisses dream.

W. Shakespeare

CXXXIII

YOUNG LOCHINVAR

O YOUNG Lochinvar is come out of the West !
Through all the wide Border his steed is the best ;
And save his good broadsword he weapon had none ;
He rode all unarm'd and he rode all alone.
So faithful in love, and so dauntless in war,
There never was knight like the young Lochinvar !

He stay'd not for brake and he stopt not for stone ;
He swam the Eske river where ford there was none ;
But ere he alighted at Netherby gate,
The bride had consented ; the gallant came late ;
For a laggard in love and a dastard in war
Was to wed the fair Ellen of brave Lochinvar.

So bravely he enter'd the Netherby Hall,
Among bridesmen and kinsmen and brothers and all.
Then spake the bride's father, his hand on his sword,
For the poor craven bridegroom said never a word,

'O come ye in peace here, or come ye in war,
Or to dance at our bridal, young Lord Lochinvar?'

'I long woo'd your daughter, my suit you denied;
Love swells like the Solway, but ebbs like its tide;
And now I am come with this lost love of mine
To lead but one measure, drink one cup of wine.
There are maidens in Scotland more lovely by far,
That would gladly be bride to the young Lochinvar!'

The bride kiss'd the goblet, the knight took it up,
He quaff'd off the wine and he threw down the cup;
She look'd down to blush, and she look'd up to sigh,
With a smile on her lips and a tear in her eye.
He took her soft hand ere her mother could bar;
'Now tread we a measure!' said young Lochinvar.

So stately his form, and so lovely her face,
That never a hall such a galliard did grace:
While her mother did fret and her father did fume,
And the bridegroom stood dangling his bonnet and
    plume;
And the bride-maidens whispered, ''T were better by
    far
To have match'd our fair cousin with young Lochinvar!'

One touch to her hand and one word in her ear,
When they reach'd the hall door; and the charger
    stood near;
So light to the croupe the fair lady he swung,
So light to the saddle before her he sprung!
'She is won! we are gone, over bank, bush, and scaur,
They'll have fleet steeds that follow!' cried young
    Lochinvar.

There was mounting 'mong Græmes of the Netherby
    clan ;
Forsters, Fenwicks, and Musgraves, they rode and they
    ran ;
There was racing and chasing on Cannobie lea ;
But the lost bride of Netherby ne'er did they see.
So daring in love, and so dauntless in war,
Have ye e'er heard of gallant like young Lochinvar !

                      Sir W. Scott

CXXXIV

INCIDENT

Characteristic of a Favourite Dog

ON his morning rounds the master
    Goes to learn how all things fare ;
Searches pasture after pasture,
Sheep and cattle eyes with care ;
And for silence, or for talk,
He hath comrades in his walk ;
Four dogs, each of a different breed,
Distinguished, two for scent, and two for speed.

See a hare before him started !
— Off they fly in earnest chase ;
Every dog is eager-hearted,
All the four are in the race !
And the hare whom they pursue
Knows from instinct what to do ;
Her hope is near, no turn she makes ;
But like an arrow to the river takes.

Deep the river was and crusted
Thinly by a one night's frost ;
But the nimble hare hath trusted
To the ice, and safely crost ;
She hath crost, and without heed
All are following at full speed,
When lo ! the ice so thinly spread,
Breaks, and the greyhound Dart is overhead !

Better fate have Prince and Swallow —
See them cleaving to the sport !
Music has no heart to follow,
Little Music, she stops short.
She hath neither wish nor heart,
Hers is now another part :
A loving creature she, and brave !
And fondly strives her struggling friend to save.

From the brink her paws she stretches,
Very hands as you would say !
And afflicting moans she fetches,
As he breaks the ice away.
For herself she hath no fears, —
Him alone she sees and hears, —
Makes efforts with complainings ; nor gives o'er,
Until her fellow sinks to re-appear no more.
W. Wordsworth

CXXXV

KING LEAR AND HIS THREE DAUGHTERS

KING Lear once ruled in this land
　　With princely power and peace ;
And had all things with heart's content,
　　That might his joys increase.
Amongst those things that nature gave,
　　Three daughters fair had he,
So princely seeming, beautiful,
　　As fairer could not be.

So on a time it pleased the king
　　A question thus to move,
Which of his daughters to his grace
　　Could show the dearest love :
'For to my age you bring content,'
　　Quoth he, 'then let me hear,
Which of you three in plighted troth
　　The kindest will appear.'

To whom the eldest thus began :
　　'Dear father mine,' quoth she,
'Before your face to do you good,
　　My blood shall render'd be :
And for your sake my bleeding heart
　　Shall here be cut in twain,
Ere that I see your reverend age
　　The smallest grief sustain.'

'And so will I,' the second said,
　　'Dear father, for your sake,

The worst of all extremities
　　I 'll gently undertake :
And serve your highness night and day
　　With diligence and love ;
That sweet content and quietness
　　Discomforts may remove.'

' In doing so, you glad my soul,'
　　The aged king replied ;
' But what say'st thou, my youngest girl,
　　How is thy love ally'd ? '
' My love,' quoth young Cordelia then,
　　' Which to your grace I owe,
Shall be the duty of a child,
　　And that is all I 'll show.'

' And wilt thou show no more,' quoth he,
　　' Than doth thy duty bind ?
I well perceive thy love is small,
　　When as no more I find.
Henceforth I banish thee my court,
　　Thou art no child of mine ;
Nor any part of this my realm
　　By favour shall be thine.

' Thy elder sisters' loves are more
　　Than I can well demand,
To whom I equally bestow
　　My kingdom and my land,
My pompal state and all my goods,
　　That lovingly I may
With those thy sisters be maintain'd
　　Until my dying day.'

Thus flattering speeches won renown
　By these two sisters here ;
The third had causeless banishment,
　Yet was her love more dear :
For poor Cordelia patiently
　Went wand'ring up and down,
Unhelp'd, unpitied, gentle maid,
　Through many an English town.

Until at last in famous France
　She gentler fortunes found ;
Though poor and bare, yet she was deem'd
　The fairest on the ground :
Where, when the king her virtues heard,
　And this fair lady seen,
With full consent of all his court,
　He made his wife and queen.

Her father, King Lear, this while
　With his two daughters stay'd :
Forgetful of their promis'd loves,
　Full soon the same decay'd ;
And living in Queen Regan's court,
　The eldest of the twain,
She took from him his chiefest means,
　And most of all his train.

For whereas twenty men were wont
　To wait with bended knee,
She gave allowance but to ten,
　And after scarce to three ;
Nay, one she thought too much for him ;
　So took she all away,
In hope that in her court, good king,
　He would no longer stay.

18

'Am I rewarded thus,' quoth he,
    'In giving all I have
Unto my children, and to beg
    For what I lately gave?
I 'll go unto my Gonorell:
    My second child, I know,
Will be more kind and pitiful,
    And will relieve my woe.'

Full fast he hies then to her court;
    Who, when she heard his moan,
Return'd him answer, that she griev'd
    That all his means were gone;
But no way could relieve his wants;
    Yet, if that he would stay
Within her kitchen, he should have
    What scullions gave away.

When he had heard with bitter tears,
    He made his answer then;
'In what I did, let me be made
    Example to all men.
I will return again,' quoth he,
    'Unto my Regan's court;
She will not use me thus, I hope,
    But in a kinder sort.'

Where when he came she gave command
    To drive him thence away:
When he was well within her court
    (She said) he would not stay.
Then back again to Gonorell
    The woful king did hie,
That in her kitchen he might have
    What scullion boys set by.

But there of that he was denied,
  Which she had promised late ;
For once refusing, he should not
  Come after to her gate.
Thus 'twixt his daughters for relief
  He wander'd up and down ;
Being glad to feed on beggar's food,
  That lately wore a crown.

And calling to remembrance then
  His youngest daughter's words,
That said the duty of a child
  Was all that love affords ;
But doubting to repair to her
  Whom he had banish'd so,
Grew frantic mad ; for in his mind
  He bore the wounds of woe :

Which made him rend his milkwhite locks
  And tresses from his head,
And all with blood bestain his cheeks,
  With age and honour spread.
To hills and woods and watery founts
  He made his hourly moan,
Till hills and woods and senseless things
  Did seem to sigh and groan.

Even thus possest with discontents,
  He passed o'er to France,
In hopes from fair Cordelia there
  To find some gentler chance ;
Most virtuous dame ! which when she heard
  Of this her father's grief,
As duty bound, she quickly sent
  Him comfort and relief :

And by a train of noble peers,
   In brave and gallant sort,
She gave in charge he should be brought
   To Aganippus' court;
Whose royal king with noble mind
   So freely gave consent
To muster up his knights at arms,
   To fame and courage bent.

And so to England came with speed,
   To repossess King Lear
And drive his daughters from their thrones
   By his Cordelia dear.
Where she, true-hearted noble queen,
   Was in the battle slain;
Yet he, good king, in his old days,
   Possest his crown again.

But when he heard Cordelia's death,
   Who died indeed for love
Of her dear father, in whose cause
   She did this battle move,
He swooning fell upon her breast,
   From whence he never parted:
But on her bosom left his life,
   That was so truly hearted.

               Old Ballad

CXXXVI

THE BUTTERFLY AND THE SNAIL

A S in the sunshine of the morn
　　A butterfly (but newly born)
Sat proudly perking on a rose,
With pert conceit his bosom glows;
His wings (all glorious to behold)
Bedropt with azure, jet, and gold,
Wide he displays; the spangled dew
Reflects his eyes and various hue.

　　His now forgotten friend, a snail,
Beneath his house, with slimy trail,
Crawls o'er the grass, whom when he spies,
In wrath he to the gardèner cries:

　　'What means yon peasant's daily toil,
From choking weeds to rid the soil?
Why wake you to the morning's care?
Why with new arts correct the year?
Why grows the peach's crimson hue?
And why the plum's inviting blue?
Were they to feast his taste design'd,
That vermin of voracious kind!
Crush then the slow, the pilfering race,
So purge thy garden from disgrace.'

　　'What arrogance!' the snail replied;
'How insolent is upstart pride!
Hadst thou not thus, with insult vain,
Provok'd my patience to complain,
I had conceal'd thy meaner birth,
Nor trac'd thee to the scum of earth;
For scarce nine suns have wak'd the hours,
To swell the fruit, and paint the flowers,

Since I thy humbler life survey'd,
In base, in sordid guise array'd.
I own my humble life, good friend;
Snail was I born and snail shall end.
And what's a butterfly?   At best
He's but a caterpillar drest;
And all thy race (a numerous seed)
Shall prove of caterpillar breed.'

J. Gay

CXXXVII

THE DÆMON LOVER

'O WHERE have you been, my long, long love,
    This long seven years and more?'
'O I'm come to seek my former vows
    Ye granted me before.'

'O hold your tongue of your former vows,
    For they will breed sad strife;
O hold your tongue of your former vows,
    For I am become a wife.'

He turn'd him right and round about,
    And the tear blinded his ee;
'I would never have trodden on Irish ground,
    If it had not been for thee.

'I might have had a king's daughter,
    Far, far beyond the sea;
I might have had a king's daughter,
    Had it not been for love of thee.'

'If ye might have had a king's daughter,
  Yourself you had to blame ;
Ye might have taken the king's daughter,
  For ye knew that I was nane.'

'O false are the vows of womankind,
  But fair is their false bodie ;
I never would have trodden on Irish ground
  Had it not been for love of thee.'

'If I was to leave my husband dear,
  And my two babes also,
O what have you to take me to,
  If with you I should go ?'

'I have seven ships upon the sea,
  The eighth brought me to land ;
With four and twenty bold mariners,
  And music on every hand.'

She has taken up her two little babes,
  Kiss'd them both cheek and chin ;
'O fare ye well, my own two babes,
  For I 'll never see you again.'

She set her foot upon the ship,
  No mariners could she behold ;
But the sails were of the taffetie,
  And the masts of the beaten gold.

She had not sail'd a league, a league,
  A league but barely three,
When dismal grew his countenance,
  And drumlie grew his ee.

The masts that were like the beaten gold
  Bent not on the heaving seas ;
And the sails that were of the taffetie
  Fill'd not in the east land breeze.

They had not sail'd a league, a league,
  A league but barely three,
Until she espied his cloven foot,
  And she wept right bitterly.

'O hold your tongue of your weeping,' says he,
  'Of your weeping now let me be ;
I will show you how the lilies grow
  On the banks of Italy.'

'O what hills are yon, yon pleasant hills,
  That the sun shines sweetly on ? '
'O yon are the hills of heaven,' he said,
  'Where you will never won.'

'O what a mountain is yon,' she said,
  ''All so dreary with frost and snow ? '
'O yon is the mountain of hell,' he cried,
  'Where you and I will go.'

And aye when she turn'd her round about,
  Aye taller he seem'd for to be ;
Until that the tops of that gallant ship
  No taller were than he.

The clouds grew dark and the wind grew loud,
  And the levin filled her ee ;
And waesome wail'd the snow-white sprites
  Upon the gurlie sea.

He struck the topmast with his hand,
  The foremast with his knee;
And he brake that gallant ship in twain,
  And sank her in the sea.

Old Ballad

CXXXVIII

THE NIGHTINGALE AND THE GLOW-WORM

A NIGHTINGALE that all day long
  Had cheer'd the village with his song,
Nor yet at eve his note suspended,
Nor yet when eventide was ended,
Began to feel, as well he might,
The keen demands of appetite;
When looking eagerly around,
He spied far off, upon the ground,
A something shining in the dark,
And knew the Glowworm by his spark;
So, stooping down from hawthorn top,
He thought to put him in his crop.
The worm, aware of his intent,
Harangued him thus, right eloquent:
'Did you admire my lamp,' quoth he,
'As much as I your minstrelsy,
You would abhor to do me wrong,
As much as I to spoil your song:
For 't was the self-same Power Divine
Taught you to sing, and me to shine;
That you with music, I with light,
Might beautify and cheer the night.'

The songster heard this short oration,
And warbling out his approbation,
Released him, as my story tells,
And found a supper somewhere else.

W. Cowper

CXXXIX

THE LADY TURNED SERVING-MAN

YOU beauteous ladies great and small,
   I write unto you, one and all,
Whereby that you may understand·
What I have suffer'd in this land.

I was by birth a lady fair,
My father's chief and only heir,
But when my good old father died,
Then I was made a young knight's bride.

And then my love built me a bower,
Bedeck'd with many a fragrant flower ;
A braver bower you ne'er did see
Than my true love did build for me.

But there came thieves late in the night,
They robb'd my bower, and slew my knight,
And after that my knight was slain
I could no longer there remain.

My servants all from me did fly
In the midst of my extremity,
And left me by myself alone
With a heart more cold than any stone.

Yet, though my heart was full of care,
Heaven would not suffer me to despair ;
Wherefore in haste I changed my name
From fair Elise to Sweet William.

And therewithal I cut my hair,
And dress'd myself in man's attire ;
And in my beaver, hose, and band,
I travell'd far through many a land.

With a silver rapier by my side,
So like a gallant I did ride ;
The thing that I delighted on,
It was to be a serving-man.

Thus in my sumptuous man's array
I bravely rode along the way ;
And at the last it chanced so
That I to the king's court did go.

Then to the king I bow'd full low,
My love and duty for to show ;
And so much favour I did crave,
That I a serving-man's place might have.

'Stand up, brave youth,' the king replied,
'Thy service shall not be denied ;
But tell me first what thou canst do ;
Thou shalt be fitted thereunto.

'Wilt thou be usher of my hall,
To wait upon my nobles all ?
Or wilt thou be taster of my wine,
To wait on me when I do dine ?

' Or wilt thou be my chamberlain,
To make my bed both soft and fine?
Or wilt thou be one of my guard?
And I will give thee thy reward.'

Sweet William, with a smiling face,
Said to the king, ' If 't please your Grace
To show such favour unto me,
Your chamberlain I fain would be.'

The king then did the nobles call,
To ask the counsel of them all ;
Who gave consent Sweet William he
The king's own chamberlain should be.

Now mark what strange thing came to pass :
As the king one day a-hunting was,
With all his lords and noble train,
Sweet William did at home remain.

Sweet William had no company then
With him at home, but an old man :
And when he saw the house was clear
He took a lute which he had there :

Upon the lute Sweet William play'd,
And to the same he sang and said,
With a sweet and noble voice,
Which made the old man to rejoice :

' My father was as brave a lord
As ever Europe did afford,
My mother was a lady bright,
My husband was a valiant knight :

' And I myself a lady gay,
Bedeck'd with gorgeous rich array ;
The bravest lady in the land
Had not more pleasure at command.

' I had my music every day,
Harmonious lessons for to play ;
I had my virgins fair and free
Continually to wait on me.

' But now, alas ! my husband 's dead,
And all my friends are from me fled ;
My former joys are pass'd and gone,
For I am now a serving-man.'

At last the king from hunting came,
And presently, upon the same,
He called for this good old man,
And thus to speak the king began :

' What news, what news, old man ?' quoth he :
' What news hast thou to tell to me ?'
' Brave news,' the old man he did say.
' Sweet William is a lady gay.'

' If this be true thou tell'st to me,
I 'll make thee lord of high degree ;
But if thy words do prove a lie,
Thou shalt be hang'd up presently.'

But when the king the truth had found,
His joys did more and more abound :
According as the old man did say,
Sweet William was a lady gay.

Therefore the king without delay
Put on her glorious rich array,
And upon her head a crown of gold
Which was most famous to behold.

And then, for fear of further strife,
He took Sweet William for his wife :
The like before was never seen,
A serving-man to be a queen.

Old Ballad

CXL

PAIRING TIME ANTICIPATED

IT chanced upon a winter's day,
  But warm, and bright, and calm as May,
The birds, conceiving a design
To forestall sweet St. Valentine,
In many an orchard, copse, and grove,
Assembled on affairs of love,
And with much twitter and much chatter,
Began to agitate the matter.
At length a Bullfinch, who could boast
More years and wisdom than the most,
Entreated, opening wide his beak,
A moment's liberty to speak ;
And, silence publicly enjoin'd,
Deliver'd briefly thus his mind :
' My friends ! be cautious how ye treat
The subject upon which we meet ;
I fear we shall have winter yet.'
   A finch, whose tongue knew no control,
With golden wing and satin poll,

A last year's bird, who ne'er had tried
What pairing means, thus pert replied :
  'Methinks the gentleman,' quoth she,
'Opposite, in the apple-tree,
By his good will would keep us single
Till yonder heaven and earth shall mingle,
Or (which is likelier to befall)
Till death exterminate us all.
I couple without more ado ;
My dear Dick Redcap, what say you ?'
  Dick heard, and tweedling, ogling, bridling,
Turning short round, strutting, and sidling,
Attested glad his approbation
Of an immediate conjugation.
Their sentiments so well express'd
Influenced mightily the rest ;
All pair'd, and each pair built a nest.
  But though the birds were thus in haste,
The leaves came on not quite so fast,
And Destiny, that sometimes bears
An aspect stern on man's affairs,
Not altogether smiled on theirs.
The wind, of late breath'd gently forth,
Now shifted east, and east by north ;
Bare trees and shrubs but ill, you know,
Could shelter them from rain and snow ;
Stepping into their nests, they paddled,
Themselves were chill'd, their eggs were addled.
Soon every father bird and mother
Grew quarrelsome, and peck'd each other.
Parted without the least regret,
Except that they had ever met,
And learn'd in future to be wiser
Than to neglect a good adviser.

W. Cowper

CXLI

TO A WATER-FOWL

WHITHER, 'midst falling dew,
    While glow the heavens with the last steps of
        day,
Far through their rosy depths, dost thou pursue
    Thy solitary way?

Vainly the fowler's eye
Might mark thy distant flight to do thee wrong,
As, darkly painted on the crimson sky,
    Thy figure floats along.

Seek'st thou the plashy brink
Of weedy lake, or marge of river wide,
Or where the rocking billows rise and sink
    On the chafed ocean side?

There is a Power whose care
Teaches thy way along that pathless coast,
The desert and illimitable air, —
    Lone wandering but not lost.

All day thy wings have fann'd,
At that far height, the cold thin atmosphere,
Yet stoop not, weary, to the welcome land,
    Though the dark night is near.

And soon that toil shall end;
Soon shalt thou find a summer home, and rest
And scream among thy fellows; reeds shall bend
    Soon o'er thy shelter'd nest.

Thou 'rt gone, the abyss of heaven
Hath swallow'd up thy form : yet on my heart
Deeply hath sunk the lesson thou hast given,
    And shall not soon depart.

He, who from zone to zone
Guides through the boundless sky thy certain flight,
In the long way that I must tread alone,
    Will lead my steps aright.

W. C. Bryant

CXLII

ROBIN HOOD AND THE BISHOP OF HEREFORD

SOME will talk of bold Robin Hood,
    And some of barons bold ;
But I 'll tell you how he served the bishop of Hereford,
    When he robbed him of his gold.

As it befell in merry Barnsdale,
    All under the greenwood tree,
The bishop of Hereford was to come by,
    With all his company.

'Come kill me a ven'son,' said bold Robin Hood,
    'Come kill me a good fat deer ;
The bishop of Hereford is to dine with me to-day,
    And he shall pay well for his cheer.

'We 'll kill a fat ven'son,' said bold Robin Hood,
    'And dress it by the highway side ;
And we will watch the bishop narrowly,
    Lest some other way he should ride.'

19

Robin Hood dressed himself in shepherd's attire,
　With six of his men also ;
And, when the bishop of Hereford came by,
　They about the fire did go.

' O what is the matter ? ' then said the bishop,
　' Or for whom do you make this ado ?
Or why do you kill the king's ven'son,
　When your company is so few ? '

' We are shepherds,' said bold Robin Hood,
　' And we keep sheep all the year,
And we are disposed to be merry this day,
　And to kill of the king's fat deer.'

' You are brave fellows,' said the bishop,
　' And the king your doings shall know :
Therefore make haste and come along with me,
　For before the king you shall go.'

' O pardon, O pardon,' said bold Robin Hood,
　' O pardon, I thee pray !
For it becomes not your lordship's coat
　To take so many lives away.

' No pardon, no pardon,' said the bishop,
　' No pardon I thee owe ;
Therefore make haste and come along with me,
　For before the king you shall go.'

Then Robin set his back against a tree,
　And his foot against a thorn,
And from underneath his shepherd's coat
　He pull'd out a bugle horn.

He put the little end to his mouth,
  And a loud blast did he blow,
Till three score and ten of bold Robin's men
  Came running all on a row.

All making obeisance to bold Robin Hood,
  'T was a comely sight for to see.
'What is the matter, master?' said Little John,
  'That ye blow so hastily?'

'O here is the bishop of Hereford,
  And no pardon we shall have.'
'Cut off his head, master,' said Little John,
  'And throw him into his grave.'

'O pardon, O pardon,' said the bishop,
  'O pardon, I thee pray!
For if I had known it had been you,
  I'd have gone some other way.'

'No pardon, no pardon,' said bold Robin Hood,
  'No pardon I thee owe;
Therefore make haste and come along with me,
  For to merry Barnsdale you shall go.'

Then Robin he took the bishop by the hand,
  And led him to merry Barnsdale;
He made him to stay and sup with him that night,
  And to drink wine, beer, and ale.

'Call in a reckoning,' said the bishop,
  'For methinks it grows wondrous high.'
'Lend me your purse, master,' said Little John,
  'And I'll tell you bye and bye.'

Then Little John took the bishop's cloak,
  And spread it upon the ground,
And out of the bishop's portmantua
  He told three hundred pound.

' Here's money enough, master,' said Little John,
  ' And a comely sight 't is to see ;
It makes me in charity with the bishop,
  Though he heartily loveth not me.'

Robin Hood took the bishop by the hand,
  And he caused the music to play ;
And he made the bishop to dance in his boots,
  And glad he could so get away.

                                        Old Ballad

CXLIII

SIR JOHN SUCKLING'S CAMPAIGN

SIR John got him an ambling nag,
  To Scotland for to ride-a,
With a hundred horse more, all his own he swore,
  To guard him on every side-a.

No errant knight ever went to fight
  With half so gay a bravado ;
Had you seen but his look, you 'd have sworn on a book
  He 'd have conquered a whole armado.

The ladies ran all to the windows to see
  So gallant and warlike a sight-a,
And as he pass'd by, they began to cry,
  ' Sir John, why will you go fight-a ? '

But he like a cruel knight spurr'd on,
  His heart did not relent-a ;
For, till he came there, he show'd no fear ;
  Till then, why should he repent-a ?

The king (Heaven bless him !) had singular hopes
  Of him and all his troop-a ;
The Borderers they, as they met him on the way,
  For joy did holloa and whoop-a.

None liked him so well as his own colonel,
  Who took him for John de Wert-a ;
But when there were shows of gunning and blows,
  My gallant was nothing so pert-a.

For when the Scots' army came within sight,
  And all men prepared to fight-a,
He ran to his tent ; they ask'd what he meant :
  He swore that his stomach ached quite-a.

The colonel sent for him back again,
  To quarter him in the van-a,
But Sir John did swear, he came not there
  To be kill'd the very first man-a.

To cure his fear he was sent to the rear,
  Some ten miles back and more a ;
Where he did play at trip and away,
  And ne'er saw the enemy more-a.

But now there is peace, he 's return'd to increase
  His money which lately he spent-a ;
But his lost honour must still lie in the dust ;
  At Berwick away it went-a.

                              Old Ballad

CXLIV

THE NUN'S LAMENT FOR PHILIP SPARROW

WHEN I remember'd again
 How my Philip was slain,
I wept and I wailed,
The tears down hailed ;
But nothing it avail'd
To call Philip again
Whom Gib our cat hath slain.
 Heu, heu, me,
That I am woe for thee !
Levavi oculos meos in montis ;
Would that I had Xenophontis
Or Socrates the Wise,
To show me their device
Moderately to take
This sorrow that I make
For Philip Sparrow's sake !
 It had a velvet cap,
And would sit on my lap,
And seek after small worms,
And sometimes white bread crumbs ;
And many times and oft
Within my breast soft
It would lie and rest.
 Sometimes he would gasp
When he saw a wasp ;
A fly or a gnat,
He would fly at that ;
And prettily he would pant
When he saw an ant ;

Lord, how he would pry
After the butterfly !
Lord, how he would hop
After the grasshop !
And when I said, Phip, Phip,
Then he would leap and skip,
And take me by the lip.
   De profundis clamavi
When I saw my sparrow die.
   Vengeance I ask and cry,
By way of exclamation,
On all the whole nation
Of cats wild and tame ;
That cat especially
That slew so cruelly
My little pretty sparrow
That I brought up at Carow.
   O cat of churlish kind,
The fiend was in thy mind.
I would thou hadst been blind !
The leopards savage,
The lions in their rage,
May they catch thee in their paws,
And gnaw thee in their jaws ;
The dragons with their tongues
May they poison thy liver and lungs.
Of India the greedy gripes
May they tear out all thy tripes ;
Of Arcady the bears
May they pluck away thine ears ;
The wild wolf Lycaon
Bite asunder thy back-bone ;
Of Ætna the burning hill,
That night and day burneth still,

Set thy tail in a blaze,
That all the world may gaze
And wonder upon thee,
From Ocean, the great sea,
Unto the Isles of Orchadye ;
From Tilbury Ferry
To the plain of Salisbury.

J. Skelton

CXLV

TO A BUTTERFLY

I 'VE watch'd you now a full half-hour,
Self-poised upon that yellow flower ;
And, little Butterfly ! indeed
I know not if you sleep or feed.
How motionless ! not frozen seas
More motionless ! and then
What joy awaits you, when the breeze
Has found you out among the trees,
And calls you forth again !

This plot of orchard-ground is ours ;
My trees they are, my sister's flowers ;
Here rest your wings when they are weary ;
Here lodge as in a sanctuary !
Come often to us, fear no wrong ;
Sit near us on the bough !
We 'll talk of sunshine and of song,
And summer days when we were young ;
Sweet childish days that were as long
As twenty days are now.

W. Wordsworth

THE DRAGON OF WANTLEY

OLD stories tell how Hercules
    A dragon slew at Lerna,
With seven heads and fourteen eyes,
    To see and well discern-a :
But he had a club, this dragon to drub,
    Or he ne'er had done it, I warrant ye :
But More of More-hall, with nothing at all,
    He slew the dragon of Wantley.

This dragon had two furious wings,
    Each one upon each shoulder ;
With a sting in his tail as long as a flail,
    Which made him bolder and bolder.
He had long claws, and in his jaws
    Four and forty teeth of iron ,
With a hide as tough as any buff,
    Which did him round environ.

Have you not heard how the Trojan horse
    Held seventy men in his belly ?
This dragon was not quite so big,
    But very near, I 'll tell ye ;
Devour'd he poor children three,
    That could not with him grapple ;
And at one sup he ate them up,
    As one would eat an apple.

All sorts of cattle this dragon would eat,
    Some say he ate up trees,
And that the forests sure he would
    Devour up by degrees :

For houses and churches were to him geese and turkeys ;
    He ate all and left none behind,
But some stones, dear Jack, that he could not crack,
    Which on the hills you will find.

Hard by a furious knight there dwelt ;
    Men, women, girls, and boys,
Sighing and sobbing, came to his lodging,
    And made a hideous noise.
O save us all, More of More-hall,
    Thou peerless knight of these woods ;
Do but slay this dragon, who won't leave us a rag on,
    We 'll give thee all our goods.

This being done, he did engage
    To hew the dragon down ;
But first he went new armour to
    Bespeak at Sheffield town ;
With spikes all about, not within but without,
    Of steel so sharp and strong,
Both behind and before, arms, legs, and all o'er,
    Some five or six inches long.

Had you but seen him in this dress,
    How fierce he look'd, and how big,
You would have thought him for to be
    Some Egyptian porcupig :
He frighted all, cats, dogs, and all,
    Each cow, each horse, and each hog :
For fear they did flee, for they took him to be
    Some strange, outlandish hedge-hog.

To see this fight all people then
    Got up on trees and houses,

On churches some, and chimneys too ;
   But these put on their trousers,
Not to spoil their hose.   As soon as he rose,
   To make him strong and mighty,
He drank, by the tale, six pots of ale
   And a quart of aqua-vitæ.

It is not strength that always wins,
   For wit doth strength excel ;
Which made our cunning champion
   Creep down into a well,
Where he did think this dragon would drink,
   And so he did in truth ;
And as he stoop'd low, he rose up and cried, boh !
   And kick'd him in the mouth.

Oh, quoth the dragon with a deep sigh,
   And turn'd six times together,
Sobbing and tearing, cursing and swearing
   Out of his throat of leather :
More of More-hall, O thou rascal,
   Would I had seen thee never ;
With the thing at thy foot thou hast prick'd my throat,
   And I 'm quite undone for ever.

Murder, murder, the dragon cried,
   Alack, alack, for grief ;
Had you but miss'd that place, you could
   Have done me no mischief.
Then his head he shaked, trembled and quaked,
   And down he laid and cried ;
First on one knee, then on back tumbled he ;
   So groan'd, and kick'd, and died.

Old Ballad

THE UNGRATEFUL CUPID

A T dead of night, when mortals lose
   Their various cares in soft repose,
I heard a knocking at my door :
'Who's that,' said I, 'at this late hour
Disturbs my rest?' It sobb'd and cried,
And thus in mournful tone replied,
'A poor, unhappy child am I,
That's come to beg your charity ;
Pray, let me in. You need not fear ;
I mean no harm, I vow and swear ;
But, wet and cold, crave shelter here ;
Betray'd by night, and led astray,
I've lost, alas ! I've lost my way.'
Moved with this little tale of fate,
I took a lamp, and oped the gate !
When, see ! a naked boy before
The threshold ; at his back he wore
A pair of wings, and by his side
A crooked bow and quiver tied.
'My pretty angel ! come,' said I,
'Come to the fire, and do not cry.'
I stroked his neck and shoulders bare,
And squeez'd the water from his hair ;
Then chafed his little hands in mine,
And cheer'd him with a draught of wine.
Recover'd thus, says he, 'I'd know,
Whether the rain has spoilt my bow ;
Let's try'—then shot me with a dart.
The venom throbb'd, did ache and smart,
As if a bee had stung my heart.

'Are these your thanks, ungrateful child,
Are these your thanks?' The impostor smiled.
'Farewell, my loving host,' says he,
'All's well; my bow's unhurt, I see;
But what a wretch I've made of thee!'

J. Hughes

CXLVIII

THE KING OF THE CROCODILES

'NOW, woman, why without your veil?
And wherefore do you look so pale?
And, woman, why do you groan so sadly,
And wherefore beat your bosom madly?'

'Oh, I have lost my darling boy,
In whom my soul had all its joy;
And I for sorrow have torn my veil,
And sorrow hath made my very heart pale.

'Oh, I have lost my darling child,
And that's the loss that makes me wild;
He stoop'd by the river down to drink,
And there was a Crocodile by the brink.

'He did not venture in to swim,
He only stoop'd to drink at the brim;
But under the reeds the Crocodile lay,
And struck with his tail and swept him away.

'Now take me in your boat, I pray,
For down the river lies my way,
And me to the Reed Island bring,
For I will go to the Crocodile King.

'He reigns not now in Crocodilople,
Proud as the Turk at Constantinople;
No ruins of his great city remain;
The Island of Reeds is his whole domain.

'Like a dervise there he passes his days,
Turns up his eyes, and fasts and prays;
And being grown pious and meek and mild,
He now never eats man, woman, or child.

'The King of the Crocodiles never does wrong,
He has no tail so stiff and strong,
He has no tail to strike and slay,
But he has ears to hear what I say.

'And to the King I will complain
How my poor child was wickedly slain;
The King of the Crocodiles he is good,
And I shall have the murderer's blood.'

The man replied, 'No, woman, no;
To the Island of Reeds I will not go;
I would not for any worldly thing
See the face of the Crocodile King.'

'Then lend me now your little boat,
And I will down the river float,
I tell thee that no worldly thing
Shall keep me from the Crocodile King.

'The King of the Crocodiles he is good,
And therefore will give me blood for blood;
Being so mighty and so just,
He can revenge me, he will, and he must.'

The woman she leapt into the boat,
And down the river alone did she float,
And fast with the stream the boat proceeds,
And now she is come to the Island of Reeds.

The King of the Crocodiles there was seen ;
He sat upon the eggs of the Queen,
And all around, a numerous rout,
The young Prince Crocodiles crawl'd about.

The woman shook every limb with fear
As she to the Crocodile King came near,
For never a man without fear and awe
The face of his Crocodile Majesty saw.

She fell upon her bended knee,
And said, ' O King, have pity on me,
For I have lost my darling child,
And that 's the loss that makes me wild.

' A crocodile ate him for his food ;
Now let me have the murderer's blood ;
Let me have vengeance for my boy,
The only thing that can give me joy.

' I know that you, sire, never do wrong,
You have no tail so stiff and strong,
You have no tail to strike and slay,
But you have ears to hear what I say.'

' You have done well,' the king replies,
And fix'd on her his little eyes ;
' Good woman, yes, you have done right ;
But you have not described me quite.

'I have no tail to strike and slay,
And I have ears to hear what you say ;
I have teeth, moreover, as you may see,
And I will make a meal of thee.'

Wicked the word, and bootless the boast,
As cruel King Crocodile found to his cost,
And proper reward of tyrannical might ;
He show'd his teeth, but he miss'd his bite.

'A meal of me !' the woman cried,
Taking wit in her anger, and courage beside ;
She took him his forelegs and hind between,
And trundled him off the eggs of the Queen.

To revenge herself then she did not fail ;
He was slow in his motions for want of a tail ;
But well for the woman was it the while
That the Queen was gadding abroad in the Nile.

Two Crocodile Princes, as they play'd on the sand,
She caught, and grasping them one in each hand,
Thrust the head of one into the throat of the other,
And made each Prince Crocodile choke his brother.

And when she had truss'd three couple this way,
She carried them off and hasten'd away,
And plying her oars with might and main,
Cross'd the river and got to the shore again.

When the Crocodile Queen came home, she found
That her eggs were broken and scatter'd around,
And that six young princes, darlings all,
Were missing ; for none of them answered her call.

Then many a not very pleasant thing
Pass'd between her and the Crocodile King;
'Is this your care of the nest?' cried she;
'It comes of your gadding abroad,' said he.

The Queen had the better in this dispute,
And the Crocodile King found it best to be mute;
While a terrible peal in his ears she rung,
For the Queen had a tail as well as a tongue.

In woful patience he let her rail,
Standing less in fear of her tongue than her tail,
And knowing that all the words which were spoken
Could not mend one of the eggs that were broken.

The woman, meantime, was very well pleased,
She had saved her life, and her heart was eased;
The justice she ask'd in vain for her son,
She had taken herself, and six for one.

'Mash-Allah!' her neighbours exclaim'd in delight,
She gave them a funeral supper that night,
Where they all agreed that revenge was sweet,
And young Prince Crocodiles delicate meat.

R. Southey

20

CXLIX

THE LION AND THE CUB

A LION cub, of sordid mind,
  Avoided all the lion kind ;
Fond of applause, he sought the feasts
Of vulgar and ignoble beasts ;
With asses all his time he spent,
Their club's perpetual president.
He caught their manners, looks, and airs ;
An ass in everything but ears !
If e'er his Highness meant a joke,
They grinn'd applause before he spoke ;
But at each word what shouts of praise ;
Goodness ! how natural he brays !

  Elate with flattery and conceit,
He seeks his royal sire's retreat ;
Forward and fond to show his parts,
His Highness brays ; the lion starts.

  ' Puppy ! that curs'd vociferation
Betrays thy life and conversation :
Coxcombs, an ever-noisy race,
Are trumpets of their own disgrace.

  ' Why so severe ? ' the cub replies ;
' Our senate always held me wise ! '

  ' How weak is pride,' returns the sire :
' All fools are vain when fools admire !
But know, what stupid asses prize,
Lions and noble beasts despise.'

J. Gay

CL

THE SNAIL

TO grass, or leaf, or fruit, or wall,
  The snail sticks close, nor fears to fall,
As if he grew there house and all
                    Together.

Within that house secure he hides,
When danger imminent betides
Of storm, or other harm besides
                    Of weather.

Give but his horns the slightest touch,
His self-collecting power is such,
He shrinks into his house with much
                    Displeasure.

Where'er he dwells, he dwells alone,
Except himself has chattels none,
Well satisfied to be his own
                    Whole treasure.

Thus hermit-like his life he leads,
Nor partner of his banquet needs,
And, if he meets one, only feeds
                    The faster.

Who seeks him must be worse than blind.
(He and his house are so combined,)
If, finding it, he fails to find
                    Its master.

                    V. Bourne

THE COLUBRIAD

CLOSE by the threshold of a door nail'd fast,
　　Three kittens sat ; each kitten look'd aghast.
I, passing swift and inattentive·by,
At the three kittens cast a careless eye ;
Not much concern'd to know what they did there,
Not deeming kittens worth a Poet's care.
But presently a loud and furious hiss
Caused me to stop, and to exclaim, 'What's this?'
When lo ! upon the threshold met my view,
With head erect, and eyes of fiery hue,
A viper, long as Count de Grasse's queue.
Forth from his head his forked tongue he throws,
Darting it full against a kitten's nose ;·
Who having never seen, in field or house,
The like, sat still and silent as a mouse :
Only projecting, with attention due,
Her whisker'd face, she asked him, 'Who are you?'
On to the hall went I, with pace not slow,
But swift as lightning, for a long Dutch hoe :
With which well arm'd I hasten'd to the spot,
To find the viper, but I found him not.
And, turning up the leaves and shrubs around,
Found only, that he was not to be found.
But still the kitten, sitting as before,
Sat watching close the bottom of the door.
'I hope,' said I, 'the villain I would kill
Has slipp'd between the door and the door-sill ;
And if I make despatch, and follow hard,
No doubt but I-shall find him in the yard';

For long ere now it should have been rehearsed,
'T was in the garden that I found him first.
Even there I found him — there the full-grown cat
His head, with velvet paw, did gently pat ;
As curious as the kittens each had been
To learn what this phenomenon might mean.
Fill'd with heroic ardour at the sight,
And fearing every moment he would bite,
And rob our household of our only cat
That was of age to combat with a rat,
With outstretch'd hoe I slew him at the door,
And taught him never to come thither more.

W. Cowper

CLII

THE PRIEST AND THE MULBERRY-TREE

DID you hear of the curate who mounted his mare,
  And merrily trotted along to the fair ?
Of creature more tractable none ever heard,
In the height of her speed she would stop at a word ;
But again with a word, when the curate said, Hey,
She put forth her mettle and gallop'd away.

As near to the gates of the city he rode,
While the sun of September all brilliantly glow'd,
The good priest discover'd, with eyes of desire,
A mulberry-tree in a hedge of wild brier ;
On boughs long and lofty, in many a green shoot,
Hung large, black, and glossy, the beautiful fruit.

The curate was hungry and thirsty to boot ;
He shrunk from the thorns, though he long'd for the
        fruit ;

With a word he arrested his courser's keen speed,
And he stood up erect on the back of his steed ;
On the saddle he stood while the creature stood still,
And he gather'd the fruit till he took his good fill.

'Sure never,' he thought, 'was a creature so rare,
So docile, so true, as my excellent mare ;
Lo, here now I stand,' and he gazed all around,
'As safe and as steady as if on the ground ;
Yet how had it been, if some traveller this way
Had, dreaming no mischief, but chanced to cry, Hey?'

He stood with his head in the mulberry-tree,
And he spoke out aloud in his fond reverie ;
At the sound of the word the good mare made a push,
And down went the priest in the wild-brier bush.
He remember'd too late, on his thorny green bed,
Much that well may be thought cannot wisely be said.

T. L. Peacock

CLIII

THE PRIDE OF YOUTH

PROUD Maisie is in the wood,
    Walking so early ;
Sweet Robin sits on the bush
    Singing so rarely.

'Tell me, thou bonny bird,
    When shall I marry me?'
'When six braw gentlemen
    Kirkward shall carry ye.'

'Who makes the bridal bed,
    Birdie, say truly?'
'The gray-headed sexton
    That delves the grave duly.

'The glow-worm o'er grave and stone
    Shall light thee steady;
The owl from the steeple sing,
    Welcome, proud lady.'

Sir W. Scott

CLIV

SIR LANCELOT DU LAKE

WHEN Arthur first in court began,
    And was approved king,
By force of arms great victories wan
    And conquest home did bring,

Then into England straight he came
    With fifty good and able
Knights, that resorted unto him,
    And were of his round table:

And he had jousts and tournaments,
    Whereto were many prest,
Wherein some knights did far excel
    And eke surmount the rest.

But one Sir Lancelot du Lake,
    Who was approved well,
He for his deeds and feats of arms
    All others did excel.

When he had rested him awhile,
    In play, and game, and sport,
He said he would go prove himself
    In some adventurous sort.

He armed rode in a forest wide,
    And met a damsel fair,
Who told him of adventures great,
    Whereto he gave great ear.

'Such would I find,' quoth Lancelot :
    'For that cause came I hither.'
'Thou seem'st,' quoth she, 'a knight full good,
    And I will bring thee thither,

'Whereas a mighty knight doth dwell,
    That now is of great fame :
Therefore tell me what wight thou art,
    And what may be thy name.'

'My name is Lancelot du Lake.'
    Quoth she, 'It likes me than ;
Here dwells a knight who never was
    Yet match'd with any man :

'Who has in prison threescore knights
    And four that he did wound ;
Knights of King Arthur's court they be,
    And of his table round.'

She brought him to a river-side,
    And also to a tree,
Whereon a copper basin hung,
    And many shields to see.

He struck so hard the basin broke ;
　　And Tarquin soon he spied :
Who drove a horse before him fast,
　　Whereon a knight lay tied.

' Sir knight,' then said Sir Lancelot,
　　' Bring me that horse-load hither,
And lay him down and let him rest ;
　　We 'll try our force together :

' For, as I understand, thou hast,
　　So far as thou art able,
Done great despite and shame unto
　　The knights of the round table.'

' If thou be of the table round,'
　　Quoth Tarquin speedily,
' Both thee and all thy fellowship
　　I utterly defy.'

' That 's overmuch,' quoth Lancelot, ' tho,
　　Defend thee bye and bye,'
They set their spears unto their steeds,
　　And each at other fly.

They couch'd their spears, (their horses ran
　　As though there had been thunder,)
And struck them each immidst their shields,
　　Wherewith they broke in sunder.

Their horses' backs brake under them,
　　The knights were both astound :
To avoid their horses they made haste
　　To light upon the ground.

They took them to their shields full fast
　Their swords they drew out then,
With mighty strokes most eagerly,
　Each at the other ran.

They wounded were and bled full sore,
　They both for breath did stand,
And leaning on their swords awhile,
　Quoth Tarquin, 'Hold thy hand,

'And tell to me what I shall ask.'
　'Say on,' quoth Lancelot, 'tho.'
'Thou art,' quoth Tarquin, 'the best knight
　That ever I did know ;

'And like a knight that I did hate :
　So that thou be not he,
I will deliver all the rest,
　And eke accord with thee.

'That is well said,' quoth Lancelot ;
　'But sith it must be so,
What knight is that thou hatest thus ?
　I pray thee to me show.'

'His name is Lancelot du Lake,
　He slew my brother dear ;
Him I suspect of all the rest :
　I would I had him here.'

'Thy wish thou hast, but yet unknown,
　I am Lancelot du Lake,
Now knight of Arthur's table round ;
　King Haud's son of Schuwake ;

'And I desire thee do thy worst.'
  'Ho, ho !' quoth Tarquin, 'tho :
One of us two shall end our lives
  Before that we do go.

'If thou be Lancelot du Lake,
  Then welcome shalt thou be.
Wherefore see thou thyself defend,
  For now defy I thee.'

They buckled then together so
  Like unto wild boars rashing ;
And with their swords and shields they ran,
  At one another slashing :

The ground besprinkled was with blood :
  Tarquin began to yield ;
For he gave back for weariness,
  And low did bear his shield.

This soon Sir Lancelot espied,
  He leapt upon him then,
He pull'd him down upon his knee,
  And, rushing off his helm,

Forthwith he struck his neck in two,
  And, when he had so done,
From prison threescore knights and four
  Delivered every one.

                              Old Ballad

CLV

THE THREE FISHERS

THREE fishers went sailing away to the west,
  Away to the west as the sun went down ;
Each thought on the woman who loved him best,
  And the children stood watching them out of the
    town ;
For men must work, and women must weep,
And there 's little to earn, and many to keep,
  Though the harbour bar be moaning.

Three wives sat up in the lighthouse tower,
  And they trimm'd the lamps as the sun went down ;
They look'd at the squall, and they look'd at the shower,
  And the night-rack came rolling up ragged and
    brown.
But men must work and women must weep,
Though storms be sudden, and waters deep,
  And the harbour bar be moaning.

Three corpses lay out on the shining sands
  In the morning gleam as the tide went down,
And the women are weeping and wringing their hands
  For those who will never come home to the town ;
For men must work and women must weep,
And the sooner 't is over, the sooner to sleep,
  And good-bye to the bar and its moaning.
                                        C. Kingsley

CLVI

ALICE FELL; OR, POVERTY

THE post-boy drove with fierce career,
 For threatening clouds the moon had drown'd;
When, as we hurried on, my ear
Was smitten with a startling sound.

As if the wind blew many ways,
I heard the sound, — and more ånd more;
It seem'd to follow with the chaise,
And still I heard it as before.

At length I to the boy call'd out;
He stopp'd his horses at the word,
But neither cry, nor voice, nor shout,
Nor aught else like it, could be heard.

The boy then smack'd his whip, and fast
The horses scamper'd through the rain;
But hearing soon upon the blast
The cry, I made him halt again.

Forthwith alighting on the ground,
'Whence comes,' said I, 'that piteous moan?'
And there a little girl I found,
Sitting behind the chaise alone.

'My cloak!' no other word she spake,
But loud and bitterly she wept,
As if her innocent heart would break;
And down from off her seat she leapt.

'What ails you, child?'— she sobb'd, 'Look here!'
I saw it in the wheel entangled,
A weather-beaten rag as e'er
From any garden scarecrow dangled.

There, twisted between nave and spoke,
It hung, nor could at once be freed;
But our joint pains unloosed the cloak,
A miserable rag indeed!

'And whither are you going, child.
To-night, along these lonesome ways?'
'To Durham,' answer'd she, half wild.
'Then come with me into the chaise.'

Insensible to all relief
Sat the poor girl, and forth did send
Sob after sob, as if her grief
Could never, never have an end.

'My child, in Durham do you dwell?'
She check'd herself in her distress,
And said, 'My name is Alice Fell;
I'm fatherless and motherless.

'And I to Durham, sir, belong.'
Again, as if the thought would choke
Her very heart, her grief grew strong;
And all was for her tatter'd cloak!

The chaise drove on; our journey's end
Was nigh; and, sitting by my side,
As if she had lost her only friends,
She wept, nor would be pacified.

Up to the tavern door we post ;
Of Alice and her grief I told ;
And I gave money to the host,
To buy a new cloak for the old :

'And let it be of duffil gray,
As warm a cloak as man can sell !'
Proud creature was she the next day,
The little orphan, Alice Fell !

W. Wordsworth

CLVII

THE FIRST SWALLOW

THE gorse is yellow on the heath,
    The banks with speedwell flowers are gay,
The oaks are budding, and, beneath,
The hawthorn soon will bear the wreath,
        The silver wreath, of May.

The welcome guest of settled Spring,
    The swallow, too, has come at last ;
Just at sunset, when thrushes sing,
I saw her dash with rapid wing,
        And hail'd her as she past.

Come, summer visitant, attach
    To my reed roof your nest of clay,
And let my ear your music catch,
Low twittering underneath the thatch
        At the gray dawn of day.

C. Smith

CLVIII

THE GRAVES OF A HOUSEHOLD

THEY grew in beauty side by side,
　　They fill'd one home with glee ; —
Their graves are sever'd far and wide, —
　　By mount, and stream, and sea.

The same fond mother bent at night
　　O'er each fair sleeping brow :
She had each folded flower in sight, —
　　Where are those dreamers now ?

One, midst the forests of the West,
　　By a dark stream is laid —
The Indian knows his place of rest,
　　Far in the cedar shade.

The sea, the blue lone sea, hath one —
　　He lies where pearls lie deep ;
He was the loved of all, yet none
　　O'er his low bed may weep. ·

One sleeps where Southern vines are drest
　　Above the noble slain :
He wrapt his colours round his breast,
　　On a blood-red field of Spain.

And one — o'er her the myrtle showers
　　Its leaves, by soft winds fann'd ;
She faded 'midst Italian flowers,
　　The last of that bright band.

And parted thus they rest who play'd
 Beneath the same green tree ;
Whose voices mingled as they pray'd
 Around one parent knee ;

They that with smiles lit up the hall,
 And cheer'd with song the hearth ! —
Alas for love ! if *thou* wert all,
 And naught beyond, O Earth !
     F. Hemans

CLIX

THE THRUSH'S NEST

WITHIN a thick and spreading hawthorn bush,
 That overhung a mole-hill large and round,
I heard from morn to morn a merry thrush
 Sing hymns of rapture, while I drank the sound
With joy ; and oft, an unintruding guest,
 I watch'd her secret toils from day to day,
How true she warp'd the moss to form her nest,
 And modell'd it within with wool and clay.
And bye and bye, like heath-bells gilt with dew,
 There lay her shining eggs as bright as flowers,
Ink-spotted over, shells of green and blue ;
 And there I witness'd, in the summer hours,
A brood of Nature's minstrels chirp and fly,
 Glad as the sunshine and the laughing sky.
     J. Clare

21

CLX

THE LAST OF THE FLOCK

I

IN distant countries have I been,
  And yet I have not often seen
A healthy man, a man full grown,
Weep in the public roads alone ;
But such a one, on English ground,
And in the broad highway, I met ;
Along the broad highway he came,
His cheeks with tears were wet ;
Sturdy he seem'd, though he was sad ;
And in his arms a lamb he had.

2

He saw me, and he turn'd aside,
As if he wish'd himself to hide :
And with his coat did then essay
To wipe those briny tears away.
I follow'd him and said, ' My friend,
What ails you ? wherefore weep you so ?
— ' Shame on me, sir ! this lusty lamb,
He makes my tears to flow.
To-day I fetch'd him from the rock ;
He is the last of all my flock.

3

' When I was young, a single man,
And after youthful follies ran,
Though little given to care and thought,
Yet so it was, an ewe I bought ;

And other sheep from her I raised,
As healthy sheep as you might see ;
And then I married, and was rich
As I could wish to be ;
Of sheep I number'd a full score,
And every year increas'd my store.

4

' Year after year my stock it grew ;
And from this one, this single ewe,
Full fifty comely sheep I raised,
As fine a flock as ever grazed !
Upon the Quantock Hills they fed ;
They throve, and we at home did thrive :
— This lusty lamb of all my store
Is all that is alive ;
And now I care not if we die,
And perish all of poverty.

5

' Six children, sir, had I to feed ;
Hard labour, in a time of need !
My pride was tamed, and in our grief
I of the parish ask'd relief,
They said I was a wealthy man ;
My sheep upon the uplands fed,
And it was fit that thence I took
Whereof to buy us bread.
' Do this ; how can we give to you,'
They cried, ' what to the poor is due ? '

6

' I sold a sheep, as they had said,
And bought my little children bread,

And they were healthy with their food ;
For me — it never did me good.
A woful time it was for me,
To see the end of all my gains,
The pretty flock which I had rear'd
With all my care and pains,
To see it melt like snow away —
For me it was a woful day.

7

' Another still ! and still another !
A little lamb, and then its mother !
It was a vein that never stopp'd —
Like blood-drops from my heart they dropp'd,
Till thirty were not left alive ;
They dwindled, dwindled, one by one ;
And I may say that many a time
I wish'd they all were gone ;
Reckless of what might come at last,
Were but the bitter struggle past.

8

' To wicked deeds I was inclined,
And wicked fancies cross'd my mind ;
And every man I chanced to see,
I thought he knew some ill of me.
No peace, no comfort could I find,
No ease within doors or without ;
And crazily and wearily
I went my work about ;
And oft was moved to flee from home
And hide my head where wild beasts roam.

9

' Sir, 't was a precious flock to me,
As dear as my own children be ;
For daily with my growing store
I loved my children more and more.
Alas ! it was an evil time ;
God cursed me in my sore distress ;
I pray'd, yet every day I thought
I loved my children less ;
And every week, and every day,
My flock it seem'd to melt away ;

10

' They dwindled, sir, sad sight to see !
From ten to five, from five to three,
A lamb, a wether, and a ewe ;
And then at last from three to two ;
And, of my fifty, yesterday
I had but only one :
And here it lies upon my arm,
Alas ! and I have none ;
To-day I fetch'd it from the rock —
It is the last of all my flock.'

W. Wordsworth

CLXI

THE ROMANCE OF THE SWAN'S NEST

LITTLE Ellie sits alone
'Mid the beeches of a meadow,
By a stream-side on the grass ;
And the trees are showering down
Doubles of their leaves in shadow
On her shining hair and face.

She has thrown her bonnet by;
And her feet she has been dipping
In the shallow waters' flow —
Now she holds them nakedly
In her hands, all sleek and dripping,
While she rocketh to and fro.

Little Ellie sits alone,
And the smile she softly useth
Fills the silence like a speech:
While she thinks what shall be done,
And the sweetest pleasure chooseth
For her future, within reach.

Little Ellie in her smile
Chooseth — 'I will have a lover,
Riding on a steed of steeds!
He shall love me without guile;
And to *him* I will discover
That swan's nest among the reeds.

'And the steed it shall be red-roan,
And the lover shall be noble,
With an eye that takes the breath,
And the lute he plays upon
Shall strike ladies into trouble,
As his sword strikes men to death.

'And the steed it shall be shod
All in silver, housed in azure,
And the mane shall swim the wind;
And the hoofs along the sod
Shall flash onward and keep measure,
Till the shepherds look behind.

' He will kiss me on the mouth
Then, and lead me as a lover,
    Through the crowds that praise his deeds ;
    And, when soul-tied by one troth,
Unto *him* I will discover
    That swan's nest among the reeds.'

Little Ellie, with her smile .
Not yet ended, rose up gaily, —
    Tied the bonnet, donn'd the shoe,
    And went homeward round a mile,
Just to see, as she did daily,
    What more eggs were with the two.

Pushing through the elm-tree copse,
Winding by the stream, light-hearted,
    Where the osier pathway leads —
    Past the boughs she stoops and stops :
Lo ! the wild swan had deserted,
    And a rat had gnaw'd the reeds.

Ellie went home sad and slow.
If she found the lover ever,
    With his red-roan steed of steeds,
    Sooth I know not ! but I know
She could never show him — never,
    That swan's nest among the reeds.

                    E. B. Browning

CLXII

SONG

I WANDER'D by the brook-side,
   I wander'd by the mill, —
I could not hear the brook flow,
   The noisy wheel was still;
There was no burr of grasshopper,
   Nor chirp of any bird;
But the beating of my own heart
   Was all the sound I heard.

I sat beneath the elm-tree,
   I watch'd the long, long shade,
And as it grew still longer
   I did not feel afraid;
For I listen'd for a foot-fall,
   I listen'd for a word, —
But the beating of my own heart
   Was all the sound I heard.

He came not, — no, he came not;
   The night came on alone;
The little stars sat one by one
   Each on his golden throne;
The evening air pass'd by my cheek,
   The leaves above were stirr'd, —
But the beating of my own heart
   Was all the sound I heard.

Fast silent tears were flowing,
   When some one stood behind;
A hand was on my shoulder,
   I knew its touch was kind:

It drew me nearer, nearer ;
   We did not speak a word, —
For the beating of our own hearts
   Was all the sound we heard.

R. M. Milnes

CLXIII

TIMOTHY

' UP, Timothy, up with your staff and away !
     Not a soul in the village this morning will stay :
The hare has just started from Hamilton's grounds,
And Skiddaw is glad with the cry of the hounds.'

Of coats and of jackets, gray, scarlet, and green,
On the slopes of the pastures all colours were seen ;
With their comely blue aprons and caps white as snow,
The girls on the hills make a holiday show.

Fresh sprigs of green box-wood, not six months before,
Fill'd the funeral basin at Timothy's door ;
A coffin through Timothy's threshold had past ;
One Child did it bear, and that Child was his last.

Now fast up the dell came the noise and the fray,
The horse and the horn, and the hark ! hark ! away !
Old Timothy took up his staff, and he shut,
With a leisurely motion, the door of his hut.

Perhaps to himself at that moment he said ;
' The key I must take, for my Ellen is dead.'
But of this, in my ears, not a word did he speak ;
And he went to the chase with a tear on his cheek.

W. Wordsworth

CLXIV

THE SLEEPING BEAUTY

I. THE MAGIC SLEEP

I

YEAR after year unto her feet,
    She lying on her couch alone,
Across the purple coverlet,
    The maiden's jet-black hair has grown,
On either side her tranced form
    Forth streaming from a braid of pearl :
The slumbrous light is rich and warm,
    And moves not on the rounded curl.

2

The silk star-broider'd coverlid
    Unto her limbs itself doth mould,
Languidly ever ; and, amid
    Her full black ringlets downward roll'd,
Glows forth each softly shadow'd arm
    With bracelets of the diamond bright :
Her constant beauty doth inform
    Stillness with love, and day with light.

3

She sleeps : her breathings are not heard
    In palace chambers far apart.
The fragrant tresses are not stirr'd,
    That lie upon her charmed heart.
She sleeps : on either hand upswells
    The gold-fringed pillow lightly press'd :
She sleeps, nor dreams, but ever dwells
    A perfect form in perfect rest.

II. THE FAIRY PRINCE'S ARRIVAL

1

A touch, a kiss ! the charm was snapt,
  There rose a noise of striking clocks,
And feet that ran and doors that clapt,
  And barking dogs, and crowing cocks ;
A fuller light illumin'd all,
  A breeze through all the garden swept,
A sudden hubbub shook the hall,
  And sixty feet the fountain leapt.

2

The hedge broke in, the banner blew,
  The butler drank, the steward scrawl'd,
The fire shot up, the martin flew,
  The parrot scream'd, the peacock squall'd,
The maid and page renew'd their strife,
  The palace bang'd and buzz'd and clackt,
And all the long pent stream of life
  Dash'd downward in a cataract.

3

And last with these the king awoke,
  And in his chair himself uprear'd,
And yawn'd, and rubb'd his face, and spoke,
  ' By holy rood, a royal beard !
How say you ? we have slept, my lords.
  My beard has grown into my lap.'
The barons swore, with many words,
  'T was but an after-dinner's nap.

4

' Pardy,' return'd the king, ' but still
  My joints are something stiff or so.

My Lord, and shall we pass the bill
    I mention'd half an hour ago?'
The chancellor sedate and vain
    In courteous words return'd reply:
But dallied with his golden chain,
    And, smiling, put the question by.

A. Tennyson

CLXV

CHORAL SONG OF ILLYRIAN PEASANTS

UP! up! ye dames, ye lasses gay!
    To the meadows trip away.
'T is you must tend the flocks this morn,
And scare the small birds from the corn.
    Not a soul at home may stay
        For the shepherds must go
        With lance and bow
To hunt the wolf in the woods to-day.

Leave the hearth and leave the house
    To the cricket and the mouse:
Find grannam out a sunny seat,
With babe and lambkin at her feet.
    Not a soul at home may stay:
        For the shepherds must go
        With lance and bow
To hunt the wolf in the woods to-day.

S. T. Coleridge

CLXVI

THE DESTRUCTION OF SENNACHERIB

THE Assyrian came down like the wolf on the fold,
　And his cohorts were gleaming with purple and
　　gold,
And the sheen of their spears was like stars on the sea,
When the blue wave rolls nightly on deep Galilee.

Like the leaves of the forest when summer is green,
That host with their banners at sunset were seen ;
Like the leaves of the forest when autumn hath blown,
That host on the morrow lay wither'd and strown.

For the Angel of Death spread his wings on the blast,
And breath'd in the face of the foe as he pass'd ;
And the eyes of the sleepers wax'd deadly and chill,
And their hearts but once heav'd, and for ever were still.

And there lay the steed with his nostrils all wide,
But through them there roll'd not the breath of his pride ;
And the foam of his gasping lay white on the turf,
And cold as the spray of the rock-beating surf.

And there lay the rider, distorted and pale,
With the dew on his brow, and the rust on his mail,
And the tents were all silent, the banners alone,
The lances unlifted, the trumpet unblown.

And the widows of Ashur are loud in their wail,
And the idols are broke in the temple of Baal,
And the might of the Gentile, unsmote by the sword,
Hath melted like snow in the glance of the Lord !
Lord Byron

CLXVII

THE WIDOW BIRD

A WIDOW bird sate mourning for her love
   Upon a wintry bough ;
The frozen wind crept on above,
   The freezing stream below.

There was no leaf upon the forest bare,
   No flower upon the ground,
And little motion in the air
   Except the mill-wheel's sound.

P. B. Shelley

CLXVIII

DORA

WITH farmer Allan at the farm abode
   William and Dora.   William was his son,
And she his niece.   He often look'd at them,
And often thought, ' I 'll make them man and wife.'
Now Dora felt her uncle's will in all,
And yearn'd towards William ; but the youth, because
He had been always with her in the house,
Thought not of Dora.
             Then there came a day
When Allan call'd his son, and said : ' My son,
I married late, but I would wish to see
My grandchild on my knees before I die :
And I have set my heart upon a match.

Now therefore look to Dora ; she is well
To look to ; thrifty too, beyond her age.
She is my brother's daughter : he and I
Had once hard words, and parted, and he died
In foreign lands ; but for his sake I bred
His daughter Dora : take her for your wife ;
For I have wish'd this marriage, night and day,
For many years.'   But William answer'd short :
'I cannot marry Dora ; by my life,
I will not marry Dora.'   Then the old man
Was wroth, and doubled up his hands, and said :
'You will not, boy ! you dare to answer thus !
But in my time a father's word was law,
And so it shall be now for me.   Look to 't ;
Consider, William ; take a month to think,
And let me have an answer to my wish ;
Or, by the Lord that made me, you shall pack
And nevermore darken my doors again !'
But William answer'd madly, bit his lips,
And broke away.   The more he look'd at her
The less he liked her ; and his ways were harsh ;
But Dora bore them meekly.   Then before
The month was out he left his father's house,
And hired himself to work within the fields ;
And half in love, half spite, he woo'd and wed
A labourer's daughter, Mary Morrison.

     Then, when the bells were ringing, Allan call'd
His niece and said : 'My girl, I love you well ;
But if you speak with him that was my son,
Or change a word with her he calls his wife,
My home is none of yours.   My will is law.'
And Dora promised, being meek.   She thought,
'It cannot be : my uncle's mind will change.'

     And days went on, and there was born a boy

To William ; then distresses came on him ;
And day by day he pass'd his father's gate,
Heart-broken, and his father help'd him not.
But Dora stored what little she could save,
And sent it them by stealth, nor did they know
Who sent it ; till at last a fever seized
On William, and in harvest-time he died.

　　Then Dora went to Mary.　Mary sat
And look'd with tears upon her boy, and thought
Hard things of Dora.　Dora came and said :
'I have obey'd my uncle until now,
And I have sinn'd, for it was all through me
This evil came on William at the first.
But, Mary, for the sake of him that 's gone,
And for your sake, the woman that he chose,
And for this orphan, I am come to you :
You know there has not been for these five years
So full a harvest : let me take the boy,
And I will set him in my uncle's eye
Among the wheat ; that, when his heart is glad
Of the full harvest, he may see the boy,
And bless him for the sake of him that 's gone.'

　　And Dora took the child, and went her way
Across the wheat, and sat upon a mound
That was unsown, where many poppies grew.
Far off the farmer came into the field
And spied her not ; for none of all his men
Dare tell him Dora waited with the child ;
And Dora would have risen and gone to him,
But her heart fail'd her ; and the reapers reap'd,
And the sun fell, and all the land was dark.

　　But when the morrow came, she rose and took
The child once more, and sat upon the mound ;
And made a little wreath of all the flowers

That grew about, and tied it on his hat
To make him pleasing in her uncle's eye.
Then when the farmer pass'd into the field
He spied her, and he left his men at work
And came and said, ' Where were you yesterday ?
Whose child is that ? what are you doing here ? '
So Dora cast her eyes upon the ground,
And answer'd softly, ' This is William's child.'
' And did I not,' said Allan, ' did I not
Forbid you, Dora ? ' Dora said again :
' Do with me as you will, but take the child
And bless him for the sake of him that 's gone.'
And Allan said : ' I see it is a trick
Got up betwixt you and the woman there.
I must be taught my duty, and by you !
You knew my word was law, and yet you dared
To slight it. Well — for I will take the boy ;
But go you hence, and never see me more.'

So saying, he took the boy, that cried aloud
And struggled hard. The wreath of flowers fell
At Dora's feet. She bow'd upon her hands,
And the boy's cry came to her from the field,
More and more distant. She bow'd down her head,
Remembering the day when first she came,
And all the things that had been. She bow'd down
And wept in secret ; and the reapers reap'd,
And the sun fell, and all the land was dark.

Then Dora went to Mary's house, and stood
Upon the threshold. Mary saw the boy
Was not with Dora. She broke out in praise
To God that help'd her in her widowhood.
And Dora said : ' My uncle took the boy ;
But, Mary, let me live and work with you :
He says that he will never see me more.'

22

Then answer'd Mary, 'This shall never be,
That thou shouldst take my trouble on thyself:
And, now I think, he shall not have the boy,
For he will teach him hardness, and to slight
His mother: therefore thou and I will go,
And I will have my boy, and bring him home;
And I will beg of him to take thee back;
And if he will not take thee back again,
Then thou and I will live within one house,
And work for William's child until he grows
Of age to help us.'
　　　　　　　　So the women kiss'd
Each other, and set out and reach'd the farm.
The door was off the latch; they peep'd and saw
The boy set up betwixt his grandsire's knees,
Who thrust him in the hollows of his arm,
And clapt him on the hands and on the cheeks,
Like one that loved him: and the lad·stretch'd out
And babbled for the golden seal that hung
From Allan's watch, and sparkled by the fire.
Then they came in; but when the boy beheld
His mother, he cried out to come to her:
And Allan sat him down, and Mary said:
'O Father! — if you let me call you so —
I never came a-begging for myself,
Or William, or this child; but now I come
For Dora: take her back; she loves you well;
O Sir, when William died, he died at peace
With all men; for I ask'd him, and he said,
He could not ever rue his marrying me.
I had been a patient wife: but, Sir, he said
That he was wrong to cross his father thus:
"God bless him!" he said, "and may he never know
The troubles I have gone through!" then he turn'd

His face and pass'd — unhappy that I am !
But now, Sir, let me have my boy, for you
Will make him hard, and he will learn to slight
His father's memory ; and take Dora back,
And let all this be as it was before.'
  So Mary said, and Dora hid her face
By Mary.   There was silence in the room,
And all at once the old man burst in sobs : —
'I have been to blame — to blame !   I have kill'd my
      son !
I have kill'd him — but I loved him — my dear son !
May God forgive me ! — I have been to blame.
Kiss me, my children !'
                        Then they clung about
The old man's neck, and kiss'd him many times,
And all the man was broken with remorse ;
And all his love came back a hundred-fold ;
And for three hours he sobb'd o'er William's child,
Thinking of William.
                        So those four abode
Within one house together ; and as years
Went forward, Mary took another mate ;
But Dora lived unmarried till her death.

                                A. Tennyson

CLXIX

A WITCH

Spoken by a Countryman

THERE 'S that old hag Moll Brown, look, see,
    just past !
I wish the ugly sly old witch
Would tumble over in the ditch ;
I would n't pick her out not very fast.
I don't think she 's belied, 't is clear 's the sun
That she 's a witch if ever there was one.
Yes, I do know just hereabout of two
Or three folk that have learnt what Moll can do.
She did, one time, a pretty deal of harm
To Farmer Gruff's folks, down at Lower Farm.
One day, you know, they happen'd to offend her,
And not a little to their sorrow,
Because they would not give or lend her
The thing she came to beg or borrow ;
And so, you know, they soon began to find
That she 'd a-left her evil wish behind.
She soon bewitch'd them ; and she had such power,
That she did make their milk and ale turn sour,
And addle all the eggs their fowls did lay ;
They could n't fetch the butter in the churn,
And cheeses soon began to turn
All back again to curds and whey.
The little pigs a-running with the sow
Did sicken somehow, nobody knew how,
And fall, and turn their snouts towards the sky,
And only give one little grunt and die ;

And all the little ducks and chicken
Were death-struck while they were a-pickin'
Their food, and fell upon their head,
And flapp'd their wings and dropp'd down dead.
They could n't fat the calves ; they would n't thrive ;
They could n't save their lambs alive ;
Their sheep all took the rot and gave no wool ;
Their horses fell away to skin and bones,
And got so weak they could n't pull
A half a peck of stones ;
The dog got dead-alive and drowsy,
The cat fell sick and would n't mousey ;
And if the wretched souls went up to bed
The hag did come and ride them all half dead.
They used to keep her out o' the house, 't is true,
A-nailing up at door a horse's shoe ;
And I 've a-heard the farmer's wife did try
To drive a needle or a pin
In through her old hard wither'd skin
And draw her blood, a-coming by ;
But she could never fetch a drop,
She bent the pin and broke the needle's top
Against her skin, you know, and that, in course,
Did only make the hag bewitch them worse.

W. Barnes

CLXX

NURSERY RHYMES

I

J ENNY Wren fell sick ;
    Upon a merry time,
In came Robin Redbreast,
    And brought her sops of wine.

Eat well of the sop, Jenny,
    Drink well of the wine ;
Thank you Robin kindly,
    You shall be mine.

Jenny she got well,
    And stood upon her feet,
And told Robin plainly
    She loved him not a bit.

Robin, being angry,
    Hopp'd on a twig,
Saying, Out upon you,
    Fye upon you, bold-faced jig !

2

There were three jovial Welshmen,
    As I have heard them say,
And they would go a-hunting
    Upon St. David's day.

All the day they hunted,
    And nothing could they find,

But a ship a-sailing,
　A-sailing with the wind.

One said it was a ship,
　The other said, nay ;
The third said it was a house,
　With the chimney blown away.

And all night they hunted,
　And nothing could they find,
But the moon a-gliding,
　A-gliding with the wind.

One said it was the moon,
　The other he said, nay ;
The third said it was a cheese,
　And half o't cut away.

3

There was an old woman, as I've heard tell,
She went to market her eggs for to sell ;
She went to market all on a market day ;
And she fell asleep on the king's highway.

There came by a pedler whose name was Stout,
He cut her petticoats all round about ;
He cut her petticoats up to the knees,
Which made the old woman to shiver and freeze.

When this little woman first did wake,
She began to shiver and she began to shake.
She began to wonder and she began to cry,
' Lauk-a-mercy on me, this is none of I :

' But if it be I, as I do hope it be,
I 've a little dog at home, and he 'll know me ;
If it be I, he 'll wag his little tail,
And if it be not I, he 'll loudly bark and wail ! '

Home went the little woman all in the dark,
Up got the little dog, and he began to bark ;
He began to bark, so she began to cry,
' Lauk-a-mercy on me, this is none of I ! '

4

If all the world was apple-pie,
　And all the sea was ink,
And all the trees were bread and cheese,
　What should we have to drink ?

5

There was a little boy and a little girl
　Lived in an alley ;
Says the little boy to the little girl,
　' Shall I, oh ! shall I ? '

Says the little girl to the little boy,
　' What shall we do ? '
Says the little boy to the little girl,
　' I will kiss you ! '

THE AGE OF CHILDREN HAPPIEST

if they had still Wit to understand it

L AID in my quiet bed in study as I were
    I saw within my troubled head a heap of thoughts
        appear,
And every thought did show so lively in mine eyes,
That now I sigh'd, and then I smiled, as cause of
    thoughts did rise.

I saw the little boy, in thought how oft that he
Did wish of God to 'scape the rod, a tall young man
    to be,
The young man eke that feels his bones with pain
    opprest,
How he would be a rich old man, to live and lie at
    rest !
The rich old man that sees his end draw on so sore,
How would he be a boy again to live so much the
    more.
Whereat full oft I smiled, to see how all those three,
From boy to man, from man to boy, would chop and
    change degree.

Earl of Surrey

CLXXII

THE NOBLE NATURE

IT is not growing like a tree
  In bulk, doth make man better be ;
Or standing long an oak three hundred year,
To fall a log at last, dry, bald, and sere ;
    A lily of a day
    Is fairer far in May,
  Although it fall and die that night —
  It was the plant and flower of Light.
In small proportions we just beauty see ;
And in short measures life may perfect be.

B. Jonson

CLXXIII

THE RAINBOW

MY heart leaps up when I behold
  A rainbow in the sky ;
So was it when my life began ;
So is it now I am a man ;
So be it when I shall grow old,
    Or let me die !
The child is father of the man ;
And I could wish my days to be
Bound each to each by natural piety.

W. Wordsworth

INDEX OF WRITERS

INDEX OF FIRST LINES